THERE MUST BE SOME WAY

OVERCOMING YOUR ADVERSITIES AND STRUGGLES TO ACHIEVE EMOTIONAL STRENGTH

KATHRYN PERCIFUL

AVIVA
PUBLISHING
New York

There Must Be Some Way: Overcoming Your Adversities and Struggles to Achieve Emotional Strength

Published by:
Aviva Publishing
Lake Placid, NY
(518) 523-1320
www.AvivaPubs.com

Address all inquiries to:

Kathryn Perciful
Kathy@ThereMustBeSomeWay.com
www.ThereMustBeSomeWay.com

ISBN: 978-1-944335-20-5
Library of Congress: 2020946788

Editors: Tyler Tichelaar and Larry Alexander, Superior Book Productions
Cover Design and Interior Book Layout: Nicole Gabriel, Angel Dog Productions

Every attempt has been made to properly source all quotes.

Printed in the United States of America
First Edition

To my father, Art Mell, (1924-2011):

> Your greatest gift to me was instilling in me the idea that I could do anything I wanted. You gave me opportunities and always cheered me on. It is an honor to pass that encouragement on to others!

To my mother, Maxine (1922-2003):

> You gave me unconditional love, even during times when I wasn't too loveable, and you always wanted the absolute best for me!

To my siblings: Patty Borst, Sandy Mell, and Arthur Mell Jr. (Jim):

> Your love, caring, and humor have carried me through some of my roughest times of struggle and setback, and our shared humor has provided some of my most favorite memories.

To Daryl Murrow, a long-time friend:

> You encouraged me to share the stories of my life, urging me on over Eggs Benedict on Friday mornings for nearly three years! I finally agreed to tackle this project, and I thank you, Daryl, for your insight and continued encouragement.

To the Guides, who have joined me in this journey:

> You have encouraged, challenged, and supported me every step of the way.

CONTENTS

A GUIDE BY YOUR SIDE

"Knowing what must be done does away with fear."

— Rosa Parks

While some people may suffer more setbacks in their lives than others, everyone has periods of difficulty. Right now, you may be facing adversity or a challenge that seems insurmountable. Perhaps you have a debilitating health issue, have lost a loved one, or are dealing with unemployment. Maybe a friend or family member is struggling with an issue (or several at once) and appears to be stuck. You may be overwhelmed by all the changes and complexities that make up your life right now.

First, the bad news: You're not unique.

Next, the good news: You are not alone.

As a woman now in her seventies, I've experienced both terrible lows and terrific highs. Even though I was a profound stutterer as a child, I became a confident woman who has run successful businesses and become a respected Toastmasters speaker. I went from being Kathy Mell, who was too scared to speak, to singing sultry siren songs as Luella Mellini on the public stage. Along the way, I met and worked with incredible mentors like Ralph Bruksos, Daryl Murrow, Lorraine Rice, Art Mell, and Rebecca Mabanglo-Major, and I enjoyed twenty years of marriage to jazz legend Jack Perciful.

For more than three years, a dear friend encouraged me to write this book. I hope it will show a light at the end of your dark tunnel. I'll share with you the strategies I discovered as I overcame my adversities.

The word "adversity" brings up visions of struggle, difficulty, hardship, and misfortune. By believing in my personal motto, "There must be some way," I discovered that adversities were actually opportunities; they were moments of *adversitunities.*

Perseverance was instrumental in surmounting all-but-impossible obstacles, and by shifting my focus from what was wrong to what could be better, my *adversitunities* helped me grow into the confident, successful person I am today.

Here are a few of the key strategies I'll discuss in this book:

- **Positive Thinking** is critical for skill building and resource development. By focusing on what to do next instead of what went wrong, you can overcome adversity.

- **Supporting Others** is also important because we can learn from each other, and it helps us feel connected and more positive about life.

- **Perseverance** is the tenacity needed to see adversity as opportunity and the belief that our actions can make a positive difference in our lives.

- **Problem-Solving** means also seeing how adversity becomes opportunity. Applying creativity to a problem is key to my belief that *there must be some way*.

- **Expressing Gratitude** generates hope and wellbeing in the face of despair and puts adversity into perspective. Gratitude gets us out of our narrow tunnel where we feel alone and allows us to focus on the people around us who have helped us and whom we can support in return.

Although you may be tempted to see me as a guru on a stage telling you what to do and when and where, I'd rather be your guide by your side. If you glean anything from this book that helps make your life better, my effort will have been worthwhile.

Throughout this book, I'll be sharing stories from my own life and asking you questions about yours. By learning the strategies I used in various experiences, you'll have tools to apply to your own situation. Hopefully, my stories will give you new insight into how you can change your own adversity into an *adversitunity*!

Are you ready to see that change in your life? Then let's begin.

Kathryn Perciful

Olympia, Washington

"Life isn't about finding yourself. Life

is about creating yourself."

— George Bernard Shaw

CHAPTER 1

FROM FREE SPIRIT TO STRUGGLE

"You were wild once. Don't let them tame you."

— Isadora Duncan

W hen I was two, the hearth of my grandparents' unlit fireplace was my stage. Grandpa Bill would lift me up and set my feet on the cold stone. Then he'd sit with Grandma Mary, while my mom and dad sat on nearby couches. Light streamed from a bank of large windows that ran the length of the living room and overlooked Washington State's Hammersley Inlet. My performances were spontaneous and uninhibited, and my audience was rapt, delighted by my sweeping gestures as I paced my stage, telling story after story in a language only I understood. My auburn curls bobbed with every turn of my head. When I paused, my family would applaud enthusiastically and I'd curtsy in my mint green dress with Swiss dots. I smiled and my family smiled right back. All that was missing was a microphone and something as sparkly as the sunlight on the waves outside.

Do you remember ever being the center of attention? Do you remember when you knew you were important and you were surrounded by people who believed in you?

Maybe that wasn't a possibility when you were younger.

Maybe you think it's not a possibility now.

Even though you may not want to be a performer, you do hold the possibility for living a spontaneous, authentic, and well-supported life. I believe in this kind of life for you because I believe in it for myself. No matter what your struggle might be, there must be some way to become who you want to be in this world. Take a moment and ask yourself:

Who could I be if my possibilities for life were bigger,

broader, and more far-reaching?

_____

_____

_____

_____

_____

_____

_____

_____

_____

_____

_____

_____

_____

_____

_____

_____

_____

As a two-year-old, I had no idea my performances brought my family together in a rare moment of peace. My parents and I lived in a small cabin a short distance from my grandparents' house. My mother stayed at home to care for me and my younger siblings. My grandfather was a forceful individual who expected others to do as he told them. He never complimented anyone, and he expected everyone around him to give more than 100 percent of their effort to any task. My father worked long hours in my grandfather's car dealership to gain his approval, and my mother attempted to get his approval, too, by controlling her four children's behavior. Even now, one phrase resounds in my memory from whenever I acted up.

"Wait until your dad comes home!" she'd shout, and I'd run to my room to hide from her.

Grandma Mary, Grandpa Bill's second wife, was very religious. She tried to coax my parents to join her Baptist congregation until my mother finally got us involved in the Lutheran Church. I imagine there were conflicts among them and yet, when I was the center of their attention, I only remember their proud expressions of delight.

We often don't realize when we have an impact on others. We feel keenly how others affect us, especially when we are young, but we often don't see how we change others' sense of the possible, too.

Maybe, just for a summer afternoon, my family felt happy and glad to be with each other. Maybe I gave them a sense of the possibility of relating to each other harmoniously. By the time I turned five, I freely roamed the area around my and my grandparents' homes. With my trusty cocker spaniel, Rover, by my side, I'd explore from the cedar forest and apple orchard all the way to an inlet of the Puget Sound where herons and ravens dove in and out in search of food. Like my room, the outdoors was quiet and peaceful.

Do you remember a place that made you feel safe when you were young?

Maybe it wasn't easy for you to feel safe.

Maybe the place wasn't real but one you found in a book or movie or song.

Take a moment and ask yourself:

What would a safe place to be myself look, feel, and smell like?

What possibilities could I imagine for myself there?

_____

_____

_____

_____

_____

_____

_____

_____

_____

_____

_____

_____

_____

_____

_____

_____

_____

_____

One day, I asked my mother to make a plate of food for Arthur Godfrey, the famous entertainer, because his show was going to be on the television soon. At the time, I believed that when I heard an airplane overhead, it meant he would come to our house to have *Arthur Godfrey Time* with us. I wanted to be sure he had lunch with us, too. A strange thing happened that day, though; my voice tightened and my vocal cords got stuck. My words shuddered in my mouth, tripping over my tongue as I tried to breathe.

"Kathy, slow down," my mother said, looking down at me. "Think about what you're going to say and then say it."

I swallowed and tried again.

"PPpppleeeesssuhhhh, mmmmmmmakkkke…" I stammered then stopped. I blinked at her. I wanted to say "Please make a sandwich for Mr. Godfrey," but I couldn't make my voice work like it had before. I didn't say anything for the rest of lunchtime and ate my sandwich in silence as I watched the show. I didn't understand what was happening to me, and my mother was impatient with my disfluency. Every time I tried to speak, the words got caught in my throat and my mother would chastise me.

"Kathy! Slow down! I can't understand you."

I didn't know what to do, so I ran away from her disapproval and stayed in my room. After that, I spoke less and less. I didn't climb on to my grandparents' hearth any more to perform. I had to be careful with what I said. Even though I knew what I wanted to say, I didn't trust my voice to handle my thoughts. I'd lost my voice to disfluency, a word I'd later learn was the technical term for stuttering.

Everyone around me spoke clearly, except Frank the Gardener. Grandpa Bill had hired Frank to maintain all of his grounds around his home since his garden was extensive and neither he nor Grandma Mary could keep it up. Frank lived on Grandpa's property in a tiny little toolshed that had been converted into living quarters. Frank's place was sparse, without a kitchen, any running water, or even a toilet. A cot took up most of the small space. Good thing Frank was a short man. He had wiry gray hair and always seemed to be happy. My siblings and I enjoyed being around him while he pruned bushes and dug weeds out of the flowerbeds. None of us really minded that Frank spoke with a Mexican accent and had a profound stutter.

That is, until I started stuttering myself.

"Don't hang around Frank, Kathy," my mother warned. "You've caught his stutter!"

I think she believed disfluency could be caught like a bad cold. Maybe she thought I'd be cured if I stopped hanging around Frank. I stayed in my room after that. It didn't seem fair that my siblings hadn't caught the stutter, too.

Looking back, it was hard to live with my mother's determined attempts to get me to speak. Not much was known about dealing with stuttering in the early '50s, and I know she did her best. More importantly, if I had not experienced the struggle in early life, my story would be quite different.

Do you remember a time when someone misunderstood your experiences and tried to make you change just by the force of their will?

What happened to your sense of possibility when you experienced someone who didn't believe in your ability?

_____

_____

_____

_____

_____

_____

_____

_____

_____

_____

_____

_____

_____

_____

_____

_____

When I grew older, I learned one of the first references to stuttering was in the Bible. Moses stuttered when God directed him to lead his people out of Egypt. I imagine anyone speaking to a deity would be nervous. Some scholars speculate that Pharaoh made Moses eat hot coals to prove his loyalty, and Moses started stuttering as a result. During the Roman Empire, stutterers were displayed in cages along the Appian Way. Travelers looking for entertainment threw coins at the language-impaired to hear them stutter. In the sixth century, specialists blamed the tongue for creating the stutter. For years, they experimented with various types of painful tongue surgeries to correct disfluency. The treatments, which typically involved carving out portions of the tongue, rarely cured the condition, and often, the stutterer bled to death. Another treatment involved placing a fork-shaped device under the tongue to provide support when speaking. Although more humane, use of the fork didn't cure stutters.

More recently, scientists believed disfluency was due to the speaker's intense fear. Many soldiers who returned from World War II with brain injuries also developed stutters. Serious advances in the study of Speech Language Impairment were made for adults, but few trickled down to pediatric health. Still, I didn't have to endure tongue surgery or fork hoists, and as time went on, my mother simply banished me to my room so she couldn't hear my repetitive sounds and vocal spasms. As I entered grade school, my stuttering moments were met with people who averted their eyes, tried to finish my sentences, or even worse, ignored me. Beyond its repetitious sounds, my disfluency was punctuated by flaring eyes and contorted facial features.

"KKKKathy," my classmates would mimic and tease, "why do you talk so funny?"

The other children avoided me, so I found myself alone during recess. I was so embarrassed about my disfluency and also frustrated because I wanted to relate to other children. I wanted to communicate what I had learned in school to my parents and grandparents, but I knew my voice was going to stop me.

My mother continued to have her own anxieties about my disfluency, and she struggled to "fix" me. After all, what would Grandpa Bill say?

Over the years, my room became my sanctuary and books

became my way to learn new perspectives. By the time I was ten or eleven, I would sit alone on my bedroom floor and read Nancy Drew mysteries. I read every novel in the series I could get my hands on; many I read more than once. Nancy was clever and observant, taking every clue into account and finding the truth of each mystery by the end. Nothing kept Nancy from her goals, even when obstacles came her way. She was persistent, resilient, and loyal to her belief that knowing the truth of a situation was out there; she just had to take each opportunity to gather the information that came her way or that she found on her own. She was an incurable optimist who never let challenges hold her back, much like my Grandpa Bill, even though he scared me sometimes.

"I believe we can turn this to our advantage," he would say when faced with a difficult situation at his car dealership.

Think of a situation that stumps you right now.

How would one of your heroes resolve it?

_____

_____

_____

_____

_____

_____

_____

_____

_____

_____

_____

_____

_____

_____

_____

_____

_____

_____

There had to be a way—a way to change how I communicated so I could be understood. Even at a young age, I wanted to live a different life. I held a clear vision of my future, one in which my voice was clear and matched word for word my thoughts. My parents and grandparents would be proud of me. I'd have many friends in school, and no one would tease me. I'd perform once again on the hearth of my grandparents' fireplace, and they would applaud every time.

There must be some way, I thought, and I was determined to find it. Because of Nancy Drew and Grandpa Bill, I knew if I concentrated on a problem, an answer would soon appear.

Later, I came to understand that my problem-solving abilities were strengthened by my coping skills. My motto became, "There must be some way." I've carried that belief in the possibility of a happy life since I was a child, and I have never given up on my vision.

Describe the way you approach life's challenges:

_____

_____

_____

_____

Changing adversity into an opportunity to create an *ad-versitunity* begins when you accept that you will experience many trials in your lifetime. Adversity comes in many different forms:

- Physical—weaknesses in the body caused by disease, poor nutrition, addiction, or accidents

- Mental—depression, anxiety, autism/Asperger's spectrum, bipolar disorder

- Emotional—low self-esteem, rage, codependency

- Social—social avoidance/awkwardness

- Spiritual—inability to connect with a Higher Power, conflicts with organized religion

- Financial—debt, income below a living wage, lack of savings

- External—natural disasters, others' choices and actions

These challenges can also compound and create even more stress and despair—a person unable to work (physical) may experience depression (mental) and find themselves in debt (financial). These complex challenges may seem insurmountable because we lose our perspective, and our vision for the future becomes distorted and narrowed. We become disappointed with our lives and our choices. Our mistakes and circumstances seem to doom us—especially when we lose hope. We may even blame others for our misfortune, rather than facing the mistakes and choices we made.

Hope is a powerful energy that inspires us to change and act on our own behalf and on behalf of others. Hope grows with positive thinking, determination, and support from others. You can succeed if you accept that adversity is inevitable; avoiding or resisting life's challenges only prolongs the pain. We can generate hope and create *adversitunities* by connecting eight key elements:

1. A Detailed Goal Statement
2. A List of Skills and Resources
3. A Network of Allies
4. An Expert
5. A Vision of Our Future Self

6. A Specific Goal Date

7. Supporting Others

8. Celebrating Success

As a child, I experienced hard times because of disfluency (causing both physical and social adversities), but I held the belief and hope for a better life by telling myself "There must be some way." This short phrase gave me the bones of a *goal statement* and a *vision* of my *future self.* As I grew older, I unconsciously and consciously sought the other elements to complement my goal statement until I could achieve my goals and live a happy life.

Perhaps you are experiencing a trial right now that you want to change.

What adverse situation would you like to turn into an *adversitunity*?

_____

_____

_____

_____

_____

Create a rough goal statement. What do you want to achieve by reading this book?

_____

_____

_____

_____

_____

What do you want your life to look like in the future? Who lives that kind of life now?

_____

_____

_____

_____

_____

"Whatever my mother's lack of understanding and limitations, she loved me and did the best she knew how. This I know without a doubt."

— Sonya Sotomayor, *My Beloved World*

CHAPTER 2

IS HELP ON THE WAY?

"That's what learning is, after all; not whether we lose the game, but how we lose and how we've changed because of it and what we take away from it that we never had before, to apply to other games. Losing, in a curious way, is winning."

— Richard Bach, *Bridge Across Forever: A True Love Story*

"I need to see Bobby F., Bobby K., and Kathy M.," announced a silver-haired, statuesque woman at the door of our third-grade classroom.

I looked around the classroom as I stood up and everyone watched the two Bobbies and me file into the hall. We trailed after the woman to a small table in the principal's office. On the table was a microphone attached to a tape recorder. Bobby F. tilted his blond head to one side and murmured to himself. Bobby K. looked down at the table and just rocked back and forth. I watched the woman tuck a stray hair behind her ear and then adjust the papers on the table in front of her.

"You will each speak into the microphone," said the woman. "Bobby K., you'll go first."

Bobby didn't respond right away, but he began to blink rapidly when she pushed the microphone in front of him.

"Bobby," she said gently, "I want you to talk into the microphone. Repeat this sentence: My name is Bobby."

Bobby roughly rubbed the back of his hand across his nose but didn't speak. His eyes blinked rapidly behind his black-framed glasses. He began with "M-m-m…." He paused. Once again, he tried. "M-m-m-i-i-i-iiii…." He repeated this sound once again, then stopped. He slumped in his chair, clearly exhausted from the stress of the last several minutes.

The silver-haired woman now turned to Bobby F. and repeated, "Say my name is Bobby." Bobby F. fidgeted in his chair.

After a moment of silence, the woman made her request again. "Bobby, say 'My name is Bobby.'" After two more coaxings with no response from Bobby F., the silver-haired woman turned to me.

I began to fidget. I didn't want her to record my voice. I didn't know the two Bobbies well, but I knew they had trouble paying attention in class. Even at age eight, I knew they had mental issues, ones that today would be labeled as "developmental disabilities." Why was I in this room with them?

"Kathy," she said after a few minutes of the second Bobby F.'s non-response, "Now it's your turn."

Before she could even slide the microphone to me, I could feel my throat begin to lock. I wanted to say, "My name is Kathy. I like my dog Rover." Instead, that halting jumpy voice came out of my mouth.

"M-m-m-muuhh n-n-n-ame-is-s-s-s, K-k-k-uh-K-k-k-uh...."

I took a breath and tried again, but my voiced locked even more. I couldn't even get my dog's name out before I ran out of breath. My cheeks felt hot as I tried to slow down like my mother had told me. Bobby F. seemed to sneer at me, and the woman took notes on a piece of paper. Finally, she told me to stop.

"Now children," she said. "I'm a speech therapist and I'm here to help you speak better. I'm going to play the recording now so you can hear what each of you sound like." She rewound the tape and let it play. I heard Bobby K.'s voice and then mine. My cheeks got hotter, and I wanted to run away. My voice sounded worse than I had imagined. Maybe I wasn't as smart as I thought. Maybe I was like the Bobbies and would never succeed in school.

The woman went on to explain how difficult it was for others to understand what we said. We needed to speak more clearly. She had us try different exercises with our mouths and tongues.

"Enunciate each word you want to speak," she said, sounding like my mother with her sing-song voice.

The more I tried to speak clearly, the worse I did, and the worse I felt, until finally, she led us back to our classroom.

Have you ever had an expert make you feel that you couldn't accomplish your dreams?

_____

_____

_____

_____

_____

_____

_____

_____

_____

_____

_____

_____

_____

_____

_____

_____

_____

_____

It was recess when we got back to class. I ran outside as soon as I could. I wanted to find someplace quiet to be alone, but I heard Sarah call after me.

"Hey, Kathy!" she said as she reached me. "What did you and the Bobbies get in trouble for?"

I tried to push past her. I didn't want to explain. My head hurt remembering my voice on the recording, and I didn't want to cry.

"N-n-n-n-u-th-th-th-in," I stammered as I picked up my pace and tried to escape the others. I just wanted to be alone. A small group of classmates gathered around Sarah, and I could hear them nervously whispering and giggling back and forth.

Every week for the next year and a half, the silver-haired woman would call for the two Bobbies and me from the door of the classroom, and we'd follow her to the microphone. Every week, I'd hear my voice replayed on tape, and I tried desperately to speak more clearly. Instead of helping me, though, those sessions just made me feel as disabled as the two Bobbies. My disfluency worsened, and I nearly stopped talking altogether.

After a while, the other children stopped asking where we

were going and ignored me, just like they ignored the two Bobbies. I was often the last person picked for a team, whether the game was baseball or dodgeball. I felt like a complete loser. After school, I did my chores and went to my room as quickly as I could to avoid my mother. I passed third grade and went on to fourth grade. Even after the sessions stopped, my voice wasn't any better, and the others still avoided me. I don't know what happened to the two Bobbies, but as I grew to be a teen, I kept my motto—"There must be some way"—in my heart.

Even though the speech therapist didn't know how to help me, I began to help myself. With a combination of persistence, resilience, determination, and problem-solving abilities, I turned my affliction into lessons to be learned. I believed there was a way for me to talk like everyone else. I just needed to figure out what to do. I knew I couldn't avoid living my life, so I started slowly and added skills as I discovered what worked best for me.

Pam was my good friend throughout elementary and high school, even though she was also very popular. She didn't mind that I was shy and introverted, and I admired how fearless she was when talking to other students and teachers. Being with her meant I belonged to a group, and she was willing to fill in for me when I couldn't answer the others quickly enough. She helped me gain self-confidence and become less fearful that others would think I was unintelligent. She even helped me ask a boy I'd known since the first grade to be my date for the Girls' Tolo Dance.

Who can you count on today to help you through rough times?

_____

_____

_____

_____

_____

_____

_____

_____

_____

_____

_____

Over time, I became more comfortable with my disfluency and identified sentences and words that caused me the most trouble. Words like "apple" and "elephant" started with soft vowels that were troublesome, as were words like "share" and "deliver" starting with consonants. If I was speaking on the phone, I would slap my face to stop my stuttering or use a different word to convey the same meaning. Word substitution kept me speaking fluidly. Sometimes I would begin with "Yes" to get my sentences started. Unfortunately, my mother didn't like me saying, "Yes, hello," when answering the phone, so she banned me from answering until I could just say "Hello." Changing the way I spoke was impossible, though, and I never got to answer the phone when she was nearby. For me, using "Yes" to start the conversation was a crutch to avoid stuttering. My mother, on the other hand, found it "just plane rude."

One of my advisors shared his story of stuttering. He said I became a walking thesaurus because I couldn't spell, which also helped people understand I was intelligent. Still, I have stumped spell check thousands of times and had to find another word—and as a writer, editor, and training developer, who also ran a weekly newspaper, I believe in using the exact word, which makes it more difficult. This is nothing compared to an actual issue, like disfluency, but I don't run into many who self-identify as a walking thesaurus. No one except my teachers knew I couldn't spell, so it held no social stigma.

What kinds of things do you avoid doing because you're afraid of others' reactions?

_____

_____

_____

_____

_____

_____

_____

_____

_____

_____

_____

_____

_____

Working around my disfluency was the best I could do at the time since my condition was viewed as a "problem" my family and teachers had to accommodate. I became very aware of how my way of speaking made people uncomfortable, and I did whatever I could to make others feel at ease, even to the point of being quiet rather than risk someone feeling uncomfortable with my halting speech.

One Sunday afternoon, my parents took my siblings and me to a fancy restaurant for dinner. I was excited to see salmon on the menu. Salmon is one of my favorite dishes. The word *salmon*, though, was particularly difficult for me with its soft "s" and "a" sounds. When the waitress came to take our order, I watched her carefully. If she seemed in a hurry, I'd have to give up on my salm-on dinner and have a hamburger instead. If she was kind, I might have a chance.

"And what would you like, miss?" she asked, pen in hand and ready. She smiled and seemed helpful.

I held my menu up to her and pointed to the salmon entrée.

"You'd like salmon, dear?" she said, perhaps a little more

slowly than usual.

"Yes," I replied as I nodded. I tried to ignore the impatient look on my mother's face.

"That comes with steamed vegetables and mashed potatoes, okay?"

I nodded again and handed her my menu. A few minutes later, I was enjoying my salmon, grateful that she hadn't looked at me as if I weren't as smart as the others in my family.

Some might say I was just making due rather than living the kind of full life non-stutterers enjoyed. I believe that, in many ways, I was fortunate to experience the challenge of disfluency at a young age because I developed skills over a long period rather than having to recover from a sudden illness or debilitating accident.

Recall a small victory you experienced.

What was the challenge, and what
did you do to overcome it?

Did you celebrate the victory? If so, how?
If not, what could you have done?

_____

_____

_____

_____

_____

_____

_____

_____

_____

_____

_____

_____

_____

_____

_____

Throughout my high school and college years, I continued to refine and perfect my coping strategies for getting through intense disfluency episodes. People only became aware of my affliction when my usual strategies failed.

On the surface, I was faring well, but on a deeper level, I allowed my disfluency to run my life. I wanted to be an English teacher, so I selected high school courses to achieve that career goal, but by the time I started college, I realized my dream was too ambitious for my ability. Young students could be cruel to teachers with unique traits like stuttering.

I changed my major from Education to Business Administration with a focus on Marketing. With my strong vocabulary and keen awareness of the power of words and images, I felt I could be successful in marketing. Sharing information in a written form would be my strength.

For the most part, I was content with my limited speaking fluency. I graduated from both high school and college. Part of me felt that life would always be a dance of avoiding problematic words and situations. In other words, I was contentedly stuck. I would always have to consider and accommodate my disfluency, and many of my early dreams were put on hold. They felt un-achievable.

Part of me, though, kept pushing forward. I would find a way to have a happy life. In my heart, I still had hope.

What dreams have you set aside because

of your fears and challenges?

_____

_____

_____

_____

_____

_____

_____

_____

_____

_____

Our hopes and dreams become our reality when we focus our skills and resources to bring them about. In the previous chapter, you wrote down a rough goal statement and a few words about how you'd like your life to be. In this chapter, you read how I developed certain skills to cope with my disfluency even though my speech therapist didn't provide resources I needed as a child. You may have skills and resources right now that can be used to reach your goal of a better life and a better way of living. Friends and colleagues could help you figure out your skills and strengths if it is difficult for you to see them in yourself.

What are your strongest skills? If you can't think of any, ask a trusted friend or colleague what they most admire about you.

_____

_____

_____

_____

_____

_____

_____

_____

_____

_____

_____

_____

_____

_____

_____

_____

What resources (big and small) do you have

that will help you reach your goal?

_____

_____

_____

_____

_____

_____

_____

_____

_____

_____

_____

_____

_____

_____

_____

_____

_____

Sometimes we can't see what we do best because it comes to us so easily. Perhaps you're skilled in cooking or organizing family activities. Perhaps people know they can count on you to help at your workplace or place of worship or in your community. These skills can be focused toward your goals and dreams.

The same can happen with resources. Financial hardship may seem difficult to overcome, but money isn't the only resource you may need to support your journey. The people you know may have resources you can tap into to reach your goals. Power tools can be borrowed, cast-off clothes can be repurposed, childcare can be shared, and most importantly, word of mouth can carry your message to a wide audience. It can be difficult to ask for help, but it's a skill that can be practiced and strengthened.

List the people closest to you who may be able to
help you change adversity into adversitunity.

_____

_____

_____

_____

_____

_____

_____

_____

_____

_____

_____

_____

_____

_____

_____

_____

_____

List the resources the people listed above

might share with you:

_____

_____

_____

_____

_____

_____

_____

_____

_____

_____

_____

_____

_____

_____

_____

_____

_____

"Hope is the only thing stronger than fear."

— Suzanne Collins, *The Hunger Games*

CHAPTER 3

CALIFORNIA, HERE I COME

"Don't dwell on what went wrong. Instead, focus on what to do next. Spend your energies on moving forward toward finding the answer."

— Denis Waitley

In 1970, after I graduated from college with my Bachelor's in Business Administration degree in hand, I moved to Oakland, California, to start a new life. I was pursuing my dream of becoming a copywriter to best use my marketing knowledge and writing skills. My uncle Harry, aunt Merle, and their two daughters, Sherry and Holly, welcomed me into their home.

I immediately applied at some of the larger advertising agencies in San Francisco, eager to start my career. I could see my dreams coming true. I visualized myself in my high heels climbing the hills with my briefcase in hand, conversing with clients about their marketing needs. I thought I had arrived!

After a few weeks without an interview, I went to an employment agency, believing it would get me that coveted copywriting job. Instead, I was placed as a cashier at a Pontiac dealership. Desperate for a job, I took the placement even though it meant putting my dreams on hold. I couldn't live with Uncle Harry and Aunt Merle forever. More importantly, I was afraid of failing and returning home to Shelton, Washington, without accomplishing any of my dreams. It was unthinkable to face my family after all I had done to leave my hometown. I had worked in my family's car dealership during the summers while I was a teenager, and I believed I could take that experience and be successful at the Pontiac dealership.

Even when our dreams don't immediately come true, we often adjust to new possibilities based on the skills we developed in the past.

What skills and abilities do you have now that support you and could carry you into new possibilities?

_____

_____

_____

_____

_____

_____

_____

_____

_____

_____

_____

_____

_____

_____

_____

_____

_____

_____

In my desperation to find a job and my confidence in my past experience, I didn't really consider the demands of the cashier position. My coping skills didn't help me when I tried to talk with an impatient customer about their final bill. Saying simple sums like $72.55 froze my throat and tongue. Pointing to the amount on an invoice seemed rude, and customers expected me to list each service and cost before they paid their bills. When customers arrived to pick up their cars, they were anxious to finish their transaction so they could get home as quickly as possible. They had little patience for my disfluent explanation of their bill. Customers would sigh and avert their eyes, tapping the counter as they grew more hostile, waiting for me to finish my stuttering episode. Any disagreements about the charges would make things worse. I had not yet developed coping skills to handle this precise activity. No word substitutions worked at that job.

My disfluency worsened. I developed severe anxiety over transaction encounters at the cashier's cage. Eventually, I was given more menial tasks at the dealership. Not only had my stuttering reappeared, but it had gotten me moved to less public positions— first accounts receivable and then leasing.

I felt defeated and thought I might never conquer the business world and use my best strengths. Not only was I not conquering the business world, but my strongest strengths were stifled.

"How did it go today?" Aunt Merle would ask when I came home each day.

"Just horrible."

Within a year, I decided I needed to find another job. Feeling defeated each day wasn't how I wanted to live my life.

How have you handled setbacks in your life?

How have you kept yourself motivated?

_____

_____

_____

_____

_____

_____

_____

I wanted to work in San Francisco at a better-paying job, one that used my creative problem-solving skills. San Francisco held a special place in my heart, not just because it was a bigger city than Shelton, where I was raised, but because I wanted to see if the cable cars really reached to the stars like in the Tony Bennett song. When I went out on a date (more about dating in the next chapter), I'd ask to see the sights instead of staying inside for dinner and a movie. One hot summer day when my date and I walked across the Golden Gate Bridge toward San Francisco, I could see for miles across the water.

Looking across the bay, I felt like my job prospects were better in San Francisco than in Oakland.

Finally, after sending my resume to an employment agency, I took a job as a marketing assistant at an export-import firm in San Francisco's industrial district. By working directly with clients rather than doing routine tasks like filing, I hoped my new job would give me more responsibility.

For the next two years, though, my career focused on typing business correspondence, putting together product information binders, and copying flyers on a mimeograph machine. Even though the job wasn't quite what I had visualized, I was still in California. I had survived the horrible job at the Pontiac dealership, and I was relieved I could afford to move to Walnut Creek— where my ground-floor, Pleasant Hill apartment was located in a quieter neighborhood near a Dunkin' Donuts.

At work, I received mail from foreign clients who refused to recognize women as capable of conducting business transactions. Business letters were often addressed to "Mr. Kathy Mell" rather than "Miss Kathy Mell," and one Christmas, I received a calendar graced with pin-up girls as if to emphasize the client's worldview.

Over time, I became frustrated and bored interacting with the same people day after day, rather than living the exciting life of a businesswoman wearing high heels and carrying a stylish briefcase to important meetings every day. Was it my disfluency that kept me from being taken seriously, or was it being a female in the early 1970s? Whatever the cause, the vision I had as a child of communicating with others was not matching up with how my life was evolving.

How do you know when you are stuck in a version of your life that isn't the same as what you envisioned?

_____

_____

_____

_____

In 1974, a well-regarded and well-established San Francisco insurance brokerage hired me as an assistant in its claims department. In San Francisco's financial district, I could wear the high heels of a businesswoman even though I was still typing, filing, and doing other administrative tasks.

With mahogany walls and the feel of established San Francisco wealth, the brokerage had better offices than any other place I had worked, and I felt like I was slowly working my way up in the world. The brokerage handled insurance policies for wealthy clients who needed coverage for their personal real estate and some of their commercial properties, like office buildings. I assisted Phyllis, the lead claims processor, in the routine management of her clients' needs. Phyllis was around my mother's age.

After a month, Phyllis went on a two-week vacation, and I took over her duties. My learning curve was steep as I fielded questions from clients who expected Phyllis' efficiency. Everything was new to me: what the insurance policies covered, how to negotiate with insurance companies for our clients' claims, how the insurance industry worked, and whom to call within insurance companies to resolve claims.

Simple claims typically involved personal property loss, while more complicated claims required in-depth research on policy coverage and limits. Situations I didn't know how to handle came up daily.

At first, I waited to solve these situations until Phyllis returned from vacation, but before she could return to work, she fell and broke her collarbone. The customers couldn't wait any longer, especially not the six to eight weeks she would need to recover. I had to address all the situations I had hidden in the bottom drawer because I didn't feel confident enough to deal with them.

One of the first claims I processed presented a quandary. A very wealthy, long-term client disputed a claim judgment on his homeowner's policy. Although he insured his home, he thought it unlikely his home would be damaged by fire so he declined the fire coverage. Unfortunately, he had a fire in his kitchen while I was covering for Phyllis, and he demanded the damage be covered, even though he didn't have fire coverage.

I wanted to figure out a solution to keep this wealthy client happy, but his policy was inadequate. His insistence made me nervous, yet I knew it would be bad for the company to give in to his bullying. I brought the claim to the insurance partner's attention, and he explained to the client why his claim couldn't be covered. Watching how this partner handled this situation, I saw how if I used his technique, I could be more comfortable in expressing my convictions.

This was when I really started using my problem-solving skills in the workplace. I believed there was a way to solve every issue that came up. Every problem became a puzzle that I not only solved but from which I learned. I developed a method for managing the many different challenges I faced each day.

First, I didn't let myself get overwhelmed when I didn't have a solution right off the bat. I kept my mindset of "There must be some way" and looked for the resources I needed. I looked for examples of what others had done before and adjusted their methods to the issue I was trying to resolve. I wrote down the steps for each solution in a notebook so I could refer to it later when a similar problem arose.

If a solution I'd used before worked on a new problem, great! If it didn't, then I gave it a rest and looked for more resources. Each time I noted the steps that worked and the ones that didn't, and soon, I could resolve issues fast and efficiently. I stayed patient with the process and allowed things to come into alignment, all the while assuring clients that their claims were processing. I helped my clients trust my handling of their claims by keeping them informed during the process.

Describe a task or job you enjoyed. What did you find fulfilling about it, and where did your creativity emerge?

When Phyllis returned, the drawer of unprocessed claims had long been emptied, and I could do more than just the filing and typing I had done before she went on vacation. Soon after she returned, she decided to retire, and I took her place. Working at this job was the most fulfilling position I had held up to that point, and I would have stayed longer if my personal life had been as fulfilling.

I did not realize for a long time that I had overcome a major life obstacle while working at that revered insurance brokerage. Once I realized how much I'd grown, it still took a while to accept and appreciate that my increased skills and capacity were permanent.

How have you solved complicated problems in the past?

How well have your solutions worked?

"Never give up, for that is just the place

and time that the tide will turn."

— Harriet Beecher Stowe

CHAPTER 4

LEARNING TO LOVE MYSELF

"Life is interesting. In the end, some of your greatest pains become your greatest strengths."

— Drew Barrymore

Even though I was making progress toward my dream career, I allowed my stuttering to select a mate. Meeting people outside of work was difficult for me. Having a desk job and no outside interests did not provide me with many dating opportunities. One night my aunt, uncle, and friends invited me to a local restaurant and bar they enjoyed. Working behind the bar was Kevin, an Irish descendant originally from Philadelphia, who, I soon learned, was a Scorpio with a glib tongue. His dark hair and quick banter made him very charismatic, and he entertained everyone sitting around the bar with jokes and stories. Best of all, his speech was perfectly fluent, and in many ways, he was someone I wished I could be. His magnetism drew me back every Friday, and between drinks and stories, we flirted. Soon we were dating.

I dated Kevin for the next two years for reasons I thought valid at the time. One, I could meet people as part of a couple and be part of a conversation without embarrassing anyone, especially myself. Later, I realized I couldn't have talked if I had wanted to because he dominated the conversation most of the time. Secondly, in the 1970s, if a woman wasn't married by the time she was thirty, she was often regarded as an undesirable old maid. I was quickly approaching twenty-nine, my dreams of conquering the business world were far from complete, and I hadn't solved my disfluency. I wasn't about to add spinster to the list.

You might be rolling your eyes at this admission, and, at this point, forty-some years later, my eyes are rolling as well. Rita Mae Brown once said, "Good judgment comes from experience, and experience comes from bad judgment." When my charming, well-spoken, gregarious bartender proposed, I was relieved and accepted. Someone wanted me and, I mistakenly believed, wanted to take care of me. Little did I know that over the next nine months, I would receive one of the greatest lessons of my life. As I went down the aisle in May 1975, I remember thinking, *Well, at least things can't get any worse. Au contraire.*

Describe a decision you made that you now realize led to a major setback. What lesson did you learn?

_____

_____

_____

_____

_____

_____

_____

_____

_____

_____

As I mentioned before, Kevin was a terrific storyteller. He managed to tell stories that seemed outrageous and, at the same time, possible. He had big dreams of leaving the bar, being his own boss, and becoming wealthy. Just before we were married, Kevin suggested we start an alarm company. A couple who often frequented the bar had an alarm systems company and offered to give Kevin their inventory. The units were small enough that he could sell them out of the back of his car. Kevin convinced them he would take the goods only if he could sell them and pay them back from the profits as time went on. The scheme seemed perfect to him, and yet, something about the arrangement didn't feel right to me.

At first, I tried to convince him it was a bad idea. I knew starting a business was hard work because I had watched my father run his car dealership. I told Kevin that starting a business took determination and required long workdays. We both had good jobs and could build our lives together, but Kevin wouldn't listen. After we married, Kevin moved into my apartment in Walnut Creek, and we ran the business out of a small, run-down office downtown.

We both kept our paying jobs and made sales calls after work. For me, this meant working an eight-hour day at the insurance agency, then working another six hours at the alarm company. Soon, I started arriving at the insurance brokerage exhausted and worn-out. I became short-tempered and impatient at the agency and often complained to Kevin about my frustrations with co-workers. One day after work, he went to the brokerage and caused a big scene while I was at the alarm company. I don't know what he said or did, but I was fired the next day.

Describe a time when you followed someone else's plans out of sense of loyalty. Which parts worked and which didn't?

_____

_____

_____

_____

_____

_____

_____

_____

_____

Looking back, I should have realized Kevin was probably drunk when he went to the brokerage. He drank a fifth of crème de menthe every night and would often pass out soon after. To make matters worse, the alarm systems we were selling didn't work very well. They were based on sound, such as glass breaking. Unfortunately, they also detected barking dogs and vehicles passing by. Our customers found them unreliable and annoying. All the alarms we sold were returned with the customer asking for their money back, but there was no money to give back. Between expenses and Kevin's drinking, the money was gone.

Kevin decided to expand the business by selling wireless alarm systems that, he was convinced, were better than the smaller systems we were selling. The systems were also more complicated, and neither of us had much electrical experience, so we couldn't do the troubleshooting when a customer had a problem.

Looking back, I wish I had been more assertive about not starting that sure-to-fail business venture, but without a day job, I felt I had no choice but to follow Kevin's plan.

Soon after we added the wireless systems, we sold one to

the Stockton Yacht Club. Even though the system was better than the smaller ones we sold, the alarm wasn't foolproof, and we had to travel to the club constantly to fix the problems. Stockton was over 100 miles away, so after we made repairs, we would find a yacht with a skipper who'd let us sleep onboard because we didn't have any money for a hotel room.

On the way home, we would stop by Aunt Merle's house to get three days' worth of food. Kevin's bar tips and the profits from the alarm business were not enough to keep us afloat. Essentially, we were living on a bartender's salary, much of which was pumped into a failing business.

One day, I arrived at our office to find Kevin pacing around angry and upset. When I asked him what had happened, he told me through gritted teeth that the restaurant where he worked had refused to purchase a fire alarm system from us. There was something in his eyes, something dangerous and determined. Sometimes when he was drunk and angry, he would throw things. I watched fearfully as he paced, wondering if I should walk out. Suddenly, he stood very still, as if deciding something; then he left without saying another word. A few days later, I heard someone had broken into the restaurant and set it on fire. I knew not to ask Kevin what had happened.

Kevin's alcoholism worsened, and the nightly rages started. One night, I woke to find his fingers around my throat, his grip slowly tightening. Afraid he would kill me if struggled, I held still and pretended to be asleep. He muttered a few words, and soon I felt his grip loosen. The bed shifted as he fell back into a deep sleep. My heart pounded in my chest as, in the darkness, I tried to understand what had brought me to this terrifying place.

What patterns led you to your current adversity?

What needs to change?

_____

_____

_____

_____

_____

_____

_____

_____

_____

_____

_____

_____

_____

_____

_____

_____

_____

Living in California gave me the chance to be out on my own without anyone watching over me. Unfortunately, that also meant no one was close enough to see the abuse I endured as Kevin's wife. His alcoholism was one problem, but the situation was compounded by his manic depression. Although he took the medicine prescribed, he also convinced his doctor I was manic-depressive, too, so he got a prescription for me, even though I never saw a doctor. Kevin's behavior was clearly erratic, but I took the medication to placate him. For weeks, I walked around in a fog and felt disconnected, until one day, the medicine ran out and we couldn't afford to get a refill. Over time, my head cleared, and I began to see how isolated I had become.

One day, I went to lunch at a local diner with my friend Marylou. I hadn't seen her in weeks, and it felt good to be away from Kevin for a while.

"How have you been?" she asked as our waitress brought our burgers and fries.

I sipped on my Coke thoughtfully, then looked her straight in the eye.

"I want to go home," I said, surprising myself with my own sense of conviction. Marylou didn't try to convince me to stay, and I called my dad that night.

"Can I borrow some money to buy a plane ticket home?"

He agreed, and I carefully made my plans while I waited for the funds. I tried not to think of myself as a failure as a wife because of what had happened with Kevin. Later, I realized I had spent my childhood feeling unlovable, so I had grasped at any chance to feel loved, even if what I received in return was really manipulation.

I wanted to go home to start over and find a way to live the life of my dreams. I was searching for a way to love myself, and I knew staying in California would end my life before I got a chance to fully live.

Describe a time when you decided to make a major change you hoped would lead to a better life:

_____

_____

_____

_____

_____

_____

_____

_____

_____

_____

_____

_____

_____

_____

_____

_____

_____

A few days after my lunch with Marylou, I waited for Kevin to pass out as he usually did in the early evening. I left with two suitcases, one full of bills to be paid and one full of clothes and unopened wedding presents. With no job and fearing for my life, I headed back to Washington. I wouldn't return to California for five years.

In July 1976, I divorced the dashing Irishman. By February 1977, the alarm business had failed. Using the bills I had taken with me, I filed for bankruptcy and moved in with my parents in

Shelton. All the dreams I had for a happy marriage, being financially solid, and doing meaningful work were totally destroyed. Instead of being a fantastically successful businesswoman, I had hit rock bottom and was once again living with my parents—the ending I feared the most.

Moving in with my parents didn't end my troubles. Every strange vehicle in my parents' driveway brought on an anxiety attack; I was afraid Kevin would find me. I already knew the physical damage of which he was capable. In my depression, I felt as if I had reached the end, with no way out in sight.

Without friends, I spent most of my time alone. After a few weeks, my mother had had enough and told me to get a job. Even though I wanted to stay home in a fetal position for the rest of my days, I got up and applied to work for the local employment agency.

I had survived my childhood and Kevin's abuse. I knew there must be some way to build a new life for myself. I knew I needed to bolster my self-esteem, so I began to put myself first. I needed to learn how to be my own person and not rely on others to make me whole.

After a couple of interviews, I got an offer from a well-established insurance agency in Seattle. Unbeknownst to me, the Seattle broker, Carl, and the San Francisco broker, Ted, were fraternity brothers. Carl called Ted and asked his opinion on my employability.

"If the asshole husband didn't follow her," Ted said, "hire her!"

What are three things you need to have a great life?

What is significant about each thing?

_____

_____

_____

_____

_____

_____

_____

_____

_____

_____

_____

_____

_____

_____

_____

_____

_____

_____

"The most courageous act is still to think for yourself. Aloud."

— Coco Chanel

CHAPTER 5

WINNING FRIENDS

"The successful man will profit from his mistakes and try again a different way."

— Dale Carnegie

As a claims processor at the Seattle insurance brokerage, I handled many interesting cases, and it was a relief to be doing work I felt successful at. The agency handled mostly medical claims and coverage for the handling of chemicals. The most notable policy we handled was insuring Seattle Slew's sperm. Seattle Slew was a famous racehorse that had won the Triple Crown in 1977.

At the agency, I could use my problem-solving skills to

help others, rather than using them to clean up after my ex-husband's schemes.

Finally, after two months of fear and disappointment, I could leave my parents' home and live on my own.

My sister Patty and I found a small studio apartment on Queen Anne Hill that I could afford. The apartment had a table and a Murphy bed, but it was so small that I had to move the table to pull down the bed. I couldn't afford a car, so I took the bus and walked up and down Seattle's steep hills to and from work.

Deflated after my divorce and bankruptcy, and still afraid I would fail again, I was moody, irritable, sullen, and overly sensitive. Even though I was grateful for the chance to support myself, my self-esteem was at an all-time low, and I was silently battling depression. I spoke as little as possible to avoid stuttering, and my attempts at communication were abrupt. In short, no one enjoyed working with me, and I gave no opportunity for anyone to become my friend. Still, I thought to myself, *There must be some way.*

How difficult is it for you to ask for help?

Who is one person you trusted in a time of need, and why did you feel you could talk to them?

_____

_____

_____

_____

_____

_____

_____

_____

_____

_____

_____

_____

_____

_____

_____

_____

I needed to learn something new to change my life. I started looking for new opportunities, but I was also careful not to just jump from one fresh thing to another. I decided to pay more attention to patterns of three; if I noticed something three times, I looked into it more carefully. At first, I paid attention to book or movie recommendations. I didn't go see a movie the first time I heard it was good; I waited until at least three people mentioned it to me; then I'd go to see it.

I found that waiting until the third mention of an activity helped me be more careful with my time and money, since both were scarce. I also found I got more out of the activity if I waited until I heard about it the third time. For instance, although I had been raised Lutheran, when I returned to Washington, I had not attended services for many years. My office manager at the insurance brokerage mentioned that she attended a Lutheran church, but it wasn't one close to where I lived. Then, on my way to work one day, I saw a Lutheran church near where I lived on Queen Anne Hill. Still, I waited until I met someone who invited me to go with them. The congregation was very welcoming, and I felt I could fit in easily.

How do you decide when to become involved with a group or activity?

_____

_____

_____

_____

_____

_____

_____

_____

_____

_____

_____

_____

_____

_____

_____

_____

Another day, I came across an ad in a business magazine for a local Dale Carnegie course. Carnegie is best known for his book *How to Win Friends and Influence People*, and the Dale Carnegie Course in Effective Speaking and Human Relations taught working professionals, college students, and adults how to apply Carnegie's principles in the workplace. I had heard of Dale Carnegie before and read the ad carefully. The possibility of learning his principles intrigued me, but I didn't do anything about the ad until a few days later when a coworker gave me a local Carnegie trainer's card.

I called and soon after, I met Bill, a Dale Carnegie trainer and salesman.

"The Carnegie Course sounds like something I'd like to try," I told him.

"Well, I'm not sure it would be a fit for you," he said, using what I would later learn was a negative pitch strategy. "But come to an introductory meeting anyway."

Bill explained that the introductory class was by invitation only, and he gave me the address of a two-story office building in downtown Seattle near the corner of 4th Avenue and University.

The course was expensive at $500; I only made $700 per month. But I made up my mind to take the course because I believe that learning self-improvement skills is the way to become a better person and succeed. My parents offered to pay the tuition as a Christmas gift since my bankruptcy had not been settled yet. I didn't accept until the bankruptcy was settled; then I eagerly invested in the course.

The trainer's directions led me to a large office with rows of tables and chairs. At the first meeting, I sat with about twenty-five other students near my age, a mix of women and men, and learned that the course ran for seven weeks. Classes were scheduled every Thursday night, and we would meet for two to three hours each session, learning and practicing Dale Carnegie's principles.

Bill gave us our first speaking assignment that first night. It seemed simple enough; he would call our name, and we would have to stand at the front of the room, say our name, and explain why we were in the class.

Student after student went to the front of the class and introduced themselves. As my turn approached, I started to tremble. My legs and hands shook, and my throat was dry. I wasn't prepared to speak that night, and I didn't know what to say. I was afraid I would stutter because I couldn't identify all the problem words that might come up during my brief speech. I didn't have any crutch words memorized. Instead, I focused on how to say my name and what I wanted from the class. Then Bill called on me to introduce myself.

Describe a time you took a risk you weren't

sure you were ready to handle.

What kind of support did you have?

_____

_____

_____

_____

_____

_____

_____

_____

_____

_____

_____

_____

_____

_____

_____

_____

I felt queasy as I approached the front of the room to stand before twenty-five people I had just met. To keep my legs from shaking, I leaned against a table at the front of the room. I took a breath, knowing it was time to sink or swim. I wanted to take the course, and introducing myself was the first step.

Within a few minutes, I had finished—without stuttering. I spoke clearly and assertively, and no one was any the wiser about my disfluency. In fact, all twenty-five people applauded me! I was relieved by their response, which gave me the courage to continue, even though I had been afraid of how others might react to my way of speaking.

We studied two books by Carnegie: *How to Win Friends and Influence People* and *How to Stop Worrying and Start Living*. I learned how to ask myself questions like, "What is the worst thing that could happen in this situation? Could I accept that worst thing? What could I do to improve the situation?" Each time I practiced the principles, I felt more and more confident in my speaking skills.

Working in a group helped me learn from others' experiences, and I saw how I could become more likeable and approachable.

Early in the class, two pens were given out for achievement: best speaker and most improved. Each pen was black with the award's insignia—they were actually mechanical pencils with erasers, rather than ink pens. We called them pens for short. The erasers were an important lesson; I learned that even though I wrote something, I could change my mind and erase it. The *pens* instilled the understanding that being able to change is a powerful skill. Over time, I received both pens, and I kept them for more than twenty years. They were tangible reminders of my successes and gave me confidence.

What small tokens/objects help you to feel

accomplished and stay motivated?

_____

_____

_____

_____

_____

_____

_____

_____

_____

_____

_____

_____

_____

_____

_____

_____

_____

I found I enjoyed appearing in front of an audience, just like when I was two years old. The applause after my mini-speeches made me feel accepted and that what I said mattered.

With each successful assignment, I scored pens for achievement. The rewards made me work harder, and I quickly learned many new interpersonal skills. My classmates and I had such a great time together that we started to meet after class at a local restaurant where we would order wine and delicious stuffed potatoes. Finally, I was with a group of people who enjoyed being with me, too.

After four weeks, I started noticing a change in my demeanor. I felt happier and more enthusiastic about life. My supervisor, Lorraine, noticed the change and complimented me on how well I handled myself in the office.

"I'd like you to give a presentation to the senior staff and brokerage owners, Kathy," she said to me one day.

The presentation went so well that Lorraine gave me more special projects, including working with a software company we contracted with to develop new software for the insurance accounts of a large client with a number of national and international companies. The software was for processing fire, health, and personal insurance claims for this major customer. The claims had to be followed closely, and managing them on paper was too cumbersome.

I primarily worked with the software company's president because she had designed the program. We met with programmers every two weeks to ensure development was on track. My job was to communicate the client's needs to the software company's president and solve complex problems with conflicting reporting needs as they arose.

Imagine you receive an award today....

What would the award represent, and why would it be meaningful to you?

_____

_____

_____

_____

_____

_____

_____

_____

_____

_____

_____

_____

_____

_____

_____

_____

_____

During the fifth week of the course, I found myself standing in the rain and in the dark at the corner of Fourth and University, waiting for the bus to take me home. My presentation that day had gone poorly. I felt like a failure and, for once, I didn't want to go out with the others. I watched my new Carnegie friends as they headed down the hill to our favorite restaurant. They looked happy and were enjoying each other's company, while I was still reliving what I thought was a poor performance. I felt like a young girl again, letting my sensitivity get the better of me.

There must be some way.

"You have a choice here," I said to myself as the bus approached. "Your life so far has not turned out as you had hoped. You can get on this bus and go back to your studio apartment and have a lonely evening—or you can join your friends down the hill."

In the snap of my fingers, I walked down the hill, the bus moving on without me.

My life had changed once more. I'd decided not to go back to my old life where I allowed failures to hold me back from having a good time with my friends. Instead, I was going to use the night as an opportunity to apply the lessons I'd been learning in class. I would do everything I could to relate positively to my peers and find our common ground with the hope I would be seen and valued as myself and not what I thought they imagined me to be.

I had a terrific night, and our friendships deepened. I became more comfortable with my classmates and successfully finished the course. Even though I don't know what if anything that night meant to them, I learned to respect myself for making the effort to be a different person.

Name someone who currently lives the life

you want for yourself.

Describe what you imagine their life is like

and how their story inspires you.

_____

_____

_____

_____

_____

_____

_____

_____

_____

_____

_____

_____

_____

_____

_____

"If you want to conquer fear, don't sit home and think about it. Go out and get busy."

— Dale Carnegie

CHAPTER 6

CONQUERING MY STUTTERING STRESSORS

"The one who falls and gets up is so much
stronger than the one who never fell."

— Roy T. Bennett

After a few years at the Seattle brokerage, I started thinking about another career change. The housing boom of the late 1970s was going strong, and residential real estate intrigued me. Following my Carnegie training, my presentation skills and self-confidence improved. Being a realtor would give me more flexibility in my schedule and income, and move me closer to my dream of being a successful, independent professional. Real estate was one of the few industries open to women at the time that afforded the kind of independence

I wanted. I passed the licensing test easily, and I looked forward to the high commissions the housing boom could provide.

I left the insurance brokerage and joined a realty agency with a large group of realtors all eager to cash in on real estate sales. I sat with forty other realtors making cold calls to homeowners, trying to convince them to list their homes.

I soon realized I couldn't use my crutch words to give specific information, such as addresses, directions, and other details. I was very embarrassed about my disfluency and often stayed in the office after hours to make my calls. I would take a roll of toilet paper and a cup of coffee to my desk, then start dialing numbers. Each time a prospective seller hung up on me because I couldn't speak clearly, I'd cry, blow my nose on a bit of toilet paper, take a sip of coffee, and try again.

My process was slow and didn't yield very good results. If I wanted to succeed in real estate sales, I'd have to learn how to control my disfluency in all situations. I recall grabbing my tongue in frustration after a particularly difficult conversation.

"*There must be some way* to make this tongue work," I

muttered to myself after a homeowner hung up on me.

Describe an obstacle that has persisted despite your best efforts.

What kept you from giving up?

_____

_____

_____

_____

_____

_____

_____

_____

_____

_____

_____

_____

_____

_____

Very soon after that epiphany, I was introduced to a speech therapy program in the northern Seattle area. Gloria, my supervisor at the realty agency, encouraged me to take advantage of the program. She gave me time off twice a week to visit Mary, the therapist at Northwest Hospital. Mary was an older woman with brown hair and a warm personality. Her kindness gave me hope that the program would work for me.

"How long will it take to become stutter-free?" I asked on the first day.

"You will never be stutter-free," Mary replied. "Our methods are most effective for children. Around the age of four, we've seen that a child's brain will sometimes work faster than their motor skills can handle. It's a genetic mutation that occurs when a fetus is between three and fifteen weeks. Unfortunately, we find that most adults don't do well in therapy because their bodies and brains can't sync up as quickly as when they were children. Many adults drop out after a few sessions out of frustration and lack of progress."

I felt my throat clench at the prospect of never being free of my disfluency.

"*There must be some way,*" I said.

Mary looked at me carefully—maybe she saw how determined I was to succeed. I had overcome so much already; I just needed a chance to change my life once more.

"Even if you complete the therapy," she replied cautiously, "it will take at least a year from the time you begin therapy to see any results."

I nodded in acceptance, and she agreed to take me on as a patient. I didn't tell Mary at the time, but I set a goal to be stutter-free by the time my family gathered for the holidays in seven months.

At my first therapy appointment, I was videotaped during a stuttering moment. I tried not to think about the two Bobbies and the grade school recordings we had made in the principal's office. When the therapist played back the videotape, I felt sick! I saw my eyes flare out and my mouth contort. No wonder people had stared at me or diverted their eyes for the past twenty-five years whenever I spoke. I felt horrible. I'd had no idea that was what I looked like during a stuttering moment.

My first exercises were focused on my eyes so they didn't flare or wander when I spoke.

"Stare straight ahead at the person you're speaking to, Kathy," Mary directed.

The exercise was difficult because I had never thought about how my face moved when I spoke. I had to focus on not letting my eyes bug out or my gaze wander. I discovered, though, that focusing on my facial muscles helped lessen my anxiety about speaking. I couldn't feel the anxiety and change the shape of my face at the same time. I discovered that self-awareness was the first key to being able to make a change.

Describe a time when focusing on a smaller goal helped you relieve anxiety in the face of a more daunting goal.

How does achieving smaller goals strengthen your confidence when tackling bigger goals?

_____

_____

_____

_____

_____

_____

_____

_____

_____

_____

_____

_____

_____

_____

Over the following weeks, we also worked on my mouth contorting when I spoke. Again, I had to notice what my face and throat muscles were doing when I stuttered. Mary taught me how to feel the way the side of my mouth would start to spasm and, instead of continuing to speak, I would stop until the spasm passed.

For homework after one therapy session, I was told to listen to others and notice their speech patterns. When I went to church the following Sunday, I paid attention to my minister, an experienced speaker, and his speech habits for the first time. In the first minutes, I counted thirteen "ums" and realized my situation was just a different speech pattern.

I wasn't a broken person.

I felt better almost immediately.

I continued to gain skills in speaking smoothly and learned different ways to speak. I learned that if my vocal cords got stuck, I could continue to make the sound until I relaxed and the sound came out. When I felt myself start to stutter, I kept repeating the sound until the word came out. When the sound of a syllable slid out with no repetitive sounds, I could relax and speak the word smoothly.

During another session, my therapist asked me to identify a hierarchy of stressors that led to my disfluency, from least to most difficult. I wrote down a total of eighteen stressors: the least stressful was "talking to strangers," while the top two were "talking on the phone" and "talking to my family."

My therapist assigned me more homework to give me the practice I needed to eliminate each stressor from my list. In my whole life, I had never been so diligent in doing my homework because I wanted to speak clearly so much. Spring turned to summer, then to fall, and over time, I learned how to let go of the coping skills I had created over my lifetime. Each assignment helped me gain the confidence and skill I needed to eliminate circumlocutions to avoid difficult words or hand gestures and running starts to make my meaning understood.

What are the three biggest stressors keeping you from achieving your goals?

Which of these stressors causes the most trouble in your life?

_____

_____

_____

_____

_____

Finally, my therapist said it was time to tackle my second-to-the-top stressor: talking on the phone.

My assignment was to call restaurants and make reservations over the phone under my own name, "Kathy Mell." As someone who likes a big challenge, I decided to place my first call to an upscale restaurant.

"Thank you for calling Roselini's," said the clerk when I called. "How may I help you?"

"Hi. I would like to make reservations for two, for six o'clock tomorrow," I said.

"Who is the reservation for?"

My heart began to beat faster. This was the moment I had been waiting for. This was the moment I had put all my training into.

"Put the reservation under Mell," I said after a moment's pause. "It's spelled eh-MMMMM-EE-eL-L."

"Could you repeat that please?"

I took a breath.

"eh-MMMMM-EE-eL-L"

Every single letter triggered a stuttering episode, but my assignment wasn't finished. Thirty minutes later, I called back to cancel the reservation and once again spell my last name.

For two weeks, I made and cancelled reservations at four or five restaurants a night until I ran out of restaurants and could finally spell my name clearly on the phone.

After tackling the stress of talking over the phone and succeeding in changing my speaking habits, I addressed my top stressor: talking to my family. Every weekend I went to Shelton to visit my parents, and I tried the new techniques I had learned by telling them about the Carnegie methods. They were both happy and supportive that I had finally let go of my coping techniques, and they were impressed by my determination.

Finally, Christmas Day arrived. The whole family was gathered at my parents' house—siblings, grandparents, parents—everyone who knew about my fluency issues since I was a child. As the gathering went on, I felt more confident talking with each person. Even though I stayed focused on how my face felt and looked to keep my expression smooth and calm, I enjoyed all the conversations and felt they flowed well and without difficulty.

After the presents were opened and the food was eaten, I found myself sitting next to Grandma Mabel.

"I haven't heard you stutter all day, Kathy," she said, patting my shoulder. "I'm so proud of you."

In that moment, I knew I had conquered my greatest stuttering stressor. I felt like I could talk to anyone, any time. Nothing was going to stop me.

What personal accomplishments give you the greatest sense of pride?

How often do you think about these accomplishments?

_____

_____

_____

_____

_____

_____

_____

_____

_____

_____

_____

The following day, though, I couldn't talk straight at all. I had worked so hard to reach my goal of being stutter-free by December 25 that I hadn't really planned for what would happen on December 26 and beyond.

Discouraged and yet still determined, I went back to therapy and continued to do my homework and strengthen my skills. It took me a few weeks to be really stutter-free, but even Mary was surprised by how quickly I was able to master all the program's techniques. She introduced me to a young man in his twenties who was just starting the program. I told him about what he could expect and encouraged him not to give up.

"You were a stutterer," he said, eyes wide with amazement.

I nodded. Mary later told me our talk inspired him to take the program seriously. By being an example of success, I provided a special kind of coaching. He didn't need rescuing; he only needed to know it was possible to speak smoothly.

Who was the last person you helped make a decision?

What was their dilemma, and how did you help?

_____

_____

_____

_____

_____

_____

_____

_____

_____

_____

_____

_____

_____

_____

_____

_____

_____

_____

Every now and then, even today, a stuttering moment might still flare up, but I no longer use childhood crutches to work around my episodes. My confidence grew with every stutter-free moment, and I am no longer concerned about my disfluency. To my surprise, other people aren't either. Decades later, people who knew me as a child will remark how amazing it is that I no longer stutter. Strangers and old friends alike no longer avert their eyes when I speak because I present myself in a calm, positive manner.

"Failure will never overtake me if my

determination to succeed is strong enough."

— Og Mandino

CHAPTER 7

WAS IT SKILL OR WAS IT LUCK?

"Shoot for the moon. Even if you miss,

you'll land among the stars."

— Norman Vincent Peale

With my newfound ability to speak fluently, it seemed as though the skies opened. Through speech therapy, I learned how to speak clearly on the phone, and I felt more comfortable as a real estate agent. Even so, my job wasn't what I imagined. Although I loved showing properties to prospective buyers and handled transactions with little effort, the real estate boom had busted. Cold-calling potential clients and trying to convince them to put their house on the market didn't feel right; I wanted enthusiastic clients who came to me to sell their properties. The business was cutthroat and isolating, even though I worked with dozens of other realtors in our office. Although I had finally found a way to step out of the shadows and begin to shine, I realized selling homes was not the career I really wanted.

After six months not selling anything, I applied as a sales representative at a computer supply company in Seattle called Advanced Computer Products (ACP). I didn't consider returning to work in insurance because I felt that would be going in the wrong direction. Instead, I decided to use my skills in a different way.

ACP had just started a security division and needed a leader with my background. I was asked if I was interested in heading the department. For the next nine months, I tried to sell access control card readers to banks for installation in their computer rooms. In the early '80s, many believed terrorists and white-collar criminals would break into unsecured computer rooms to wreak havoc on bank computer systems.

What are your particular skills and passions?

**How could you apply these unique attributes
right now in your town, state, or country, either
as a professional or as a volunteer?**

_____

_____

_____

_____

_____

_____

_____

_____

_____

_____

_____

_____

_____

_____

_____

After limited success selling ACP card reader systems, I did some research and discovered the systems were typically bought during construction, rather than being installed in existing buildings as we had been selling them. New office buildings and parking garages were the best markets. This meant we had to secure contracts years in advance, but final sales would not produce revenue until installation.

Even so, Carolyn, my coworker, and I were interested in forming a company to meet the new market demand. Roger, the company owner, was also interested in having a separate company, so he agreed to be a third partner in the venture.

Our new company took over the sale and installation of access and parking control systems so ACP could focus on its established business. Roger was an open, energetic man who took good care of his employees.

For about a year, the arrangement seemed ideal, since Carolyn was familiar with computer security and Roger was able to find good leads on new construction projects. Over time, though, they both left the business. Roger felt the sales cycle was too long, and Carolyn was more comfortable as an employee than a business partner.

I was left alone with Sandy, our part-time receptionist. As the company's sole owner, I met with clients and provided specifications for upcoming security bids. I also drew wiring diagrams for electricians to use during installation and performed troubleshooting when systems malfunctioned after installation.

I soon acquired a maintenance contract with Puget Power to protect the transformer areas at its new administrative offices. Puget Power believed the transformers were vulnerable to terrorist attack, and the resulting contract was large enough that I hired a full-time employee exclusively responsible for maintaining Puget Power's systems and installations.

Have you ever had a lucky break?

What do you think luck is?

_____

_____

_____

_____

_____

_____

_____

_____

_____

_____

_____

_____

_____

_____

_____

_____

Some may think I was lucky to get that contract, but after all the companies I had worked for, I learned luck is more complicated than just being at the right place at the right time. You can't force luck, but I discovered that when my goals, resources, and creativity aligned, lucky things happened. My motto, "*There must be some way,*" kept me open to new possibilities and gave me the persistence to continue when in doubt. Because of my speech therapy and Dale Carnegie training, I had a good sense of my worth and the values I held dearest. Even though I was in my mid-thirties, I often felt I did not know when I would achieve my goals. Still, I believed that whatever I needed would emerge so I could take the next step in my journey.

With the increase in business came longer hours at work. I became overwhelmed with my sixty-hour workweek. I didn't want to close the business; however, I was committed to going forward and creating a strong company. I wanted to build a business that provided a good quality life for me and my employees, and I had customers who counted on me to deliver what we had promised. I realized I needed to gain skills beyond attracting new customers, formulating bids, and selling products. I needed to gain management and operations skills to ensure my business was growing and stable.

I looked for professional guidance to help me in this next stage of my career. Since it was my experience that people showed up precisely when I needed them, I wasn't surprised when Roger mentioned Ralph Bruksos to me in 1982. Ralph was—and still is—a trainer and management consultant for several Fortune 100 companies, and Ralph believed he could teach me the organizational skills I sought.

I learned Ralph had gone from being an alcoholic at age fifteen to being president and CEO of a multi-million-dollar company to being broke again. He had reinvented himself and regained his prosperity, not only in business but his personal life. He took those experiences and created a method for business people to examine their own best practices, identify what was valid in their changing market, and open themselves to new perspectives.

Over the next four years, I met with Ralph regularly. He provided an avenue for brainstorming ideas to solve problems from time management to hiring and firing employees. He guided

me through learning the best practices for conflict resolution and
creating better sales presentations.

What does success look like to you?

_____

_____

_____

_____

_____

_____

_____

_____

_____

_____

_____

_____

_____

_____

Ralph also helped me understand that my belief that as the company owner, I was always right was actually wrong and held my company back. He showed me how the most difficult, rude, and mean-spirited people could be my greatest teachers; I wanted to be a good employer and businessperson, and their examples showed me how *not* to be.

Ralph's lessons went beyond best business practices to make the rest of my life better, too.

Once, on my way to see Ralph, I drove down a back alley in Bellevue to reach the parking garage. A surly man in a beat-up Chevy truck drove past me as we tried to negotiate the narrow space. He flipped me his middle finger, and I flipped my middle finger right back. He jammed on his brakes, and I realized his rifle was resting in his truck's gun rack. Terrified, I drove away as quickly as I could and made it to the garage safe and sound. By the time I met with Ralph, my heart was racing, and I felt flustered and still very angry. I rattled off the story of the old man and his rifle and expected Ralph would be angry too.

"I don't know what he was doing in that alley!" I exclaimed.

Ralph smiled and took in a calm breath.

"Everybody has the right to be someplace," he replied.

His answer took me by such surprise. I took a step back and thought about what he was trying to teach me. I realized my mind had been closed to the possibility that the other driver was just as frightened as I was about the narrow alley. Perhaps he was startled that I was driving in the opposite direction and could hit him if I wasn't careful.

"I guess that guy could have a different view of what happened," I ventured. Ralph nodded. After that, I checked my anger whenever it flared up. I tried to keep an open mind about everyone's circumstances and take conflicts less personally.

Most importantly, Ralph taught me the importance of helping others through changes in business and their personal lives. I felt accountable to him and relied on his eloquent, non-judgmental way of telling me when I was off track with my business or advising me on how to handle a difficult situation. He had made it his life's work to study change in his own life, and he had taught me—and thousands of others—how to manage change.

With Ralph's mentorship, I was able to grow and strengthen my company over the next several years. I gained confidence in the face of change and created a business organization method that fit my values in a profitable way. When it was time for the next chapter in my life, Ralph helped me sell my business to my employees, something I had kept in mind even as I built the business. I didn't want to just close the business and leave them to find other jobs. I felt proud and delighted that they wanted to continue the company. In fact, twenty years later, they were able to sell the business to an international firm at a healthy profit. To this very day, Ralph's book, *It's Time to Move On*, inspires me to make many changes and live a fuller life.

Whom do you most admire?

What three characteristics do they possess that you admire?

_____

_____

_____

_____

_____

_____

_____

_____

_____

_____

_____

_____

_____

_____

_____

_____

_____

_____

After selling the access control business in 1986, I looked for opportunities to build and foster a business in my hometown. My father owned a petroleum distributorship, Olympia Oil and Wood, that appeared to be on the decline and looked like just the challenge I sought. First, I started with a smaller project: selling commercial property the company owned. Although Olympia Oil and Wood hadn't sold wood products since the 1950s and gasoline distribution had been added, my father and brother ran a successful asphalt plant on this commercial site for many years. The economy shifted, however, as the local population grew, and soon a new retail mall was built across the street. I devoted myself to finding someone interested in building a retail business where the old asphalt plant was. Every day I worked on creating a list of possible businesses, placed calls, and sent out information about the property. Soon, Toys "R" Us purchased the property, and we saved the profits from the property sale for another business venture that would bring profit to the fuel division once again. Then I focused my attention on the gasoline sales and delivery division. We sold and delivered Texaco gasoline to a number of Texaco stations in the Olympia area. A number of our customer stations were being taken by competing distributors or Texaco Corporate. Dad was considering closing the petroleum division because it was losing money each year. It was just the challenge I was looking for. I spent the next nine months learning everything I could about the petroleum business and, in particular, how competing distributors ran their operations. At a week-long class that all of our competitors attended, I asked one of the attendees what he thought my chances were in turning our company around. His reply was "You're fifteen years too late." Little did he realize that comment was just the challenge I needed.

When I asked Dad for the opportunity to become more involved with Olympia Oil and Wood, he granted my request. During that nine-month internship, I discovered a number of long-term employees were still using methods they had adopted in the '50s and '60s. Payroll and accounting were managed by hand. The office manager typically arrived late, only later to fall asleep at his desk. One fueling site manager was good at taking orders but couldn't make his own decisions.

At first, I tried to improve the business by taking advantage of the opportunities additional fueling sites provided, but I faced an attitude of "Well, we have always done it this way," from the company's older members. However, one key to business success, I had learned, was persistence. Eventually, I was able to computerize the payroll and accounting system. The old staff members were reluctant to move with the changes I implemented, so I found myself in conflict with them. Despite my effort to create an office culture like I had fostered at the access control firm, I soon learned that, for some employees, it was easier to watch a business fail than to make the effort to improve their methods.

One day, the office manager left on his boat for a month-long vacation. While he was gone, the bank called to inform us the company was overdrawn by almost $270,000. Both the Federal and State tax authorities had simultaneously withdrawn the petroleum taxes owed for the period. When I researched what had happened, I quickly realized the office manager had not accurately projected cash flow, even though millions of dollars were moving through monthly.

Because the office manager was a long-term employee, even though his job performance was poor, my father trusted him. I carefully scripted my conversation with my father before meeting with him to ask for a loan to cover the overdraft. I felt sick to my stomach as I explained what had happened. When the office manager returned, he was fired on the spot.

By that time, the accountant and general manager of the

existing fueling division retired and two others left because they couldn't accept the changes the new business had wrought.

The company could not survive under such stressful conditions, and I knew it needed better leadership.

Which of your skills or talents have you used in difficult work situations?

Where might you use these skills more often?

_____

_____

_____

_____

_____

_____

_____

_____

_____

_____

_____

_____

_____

_____

_____

_____

_____

Once the old-timers had left, I became general manager of the entire fuel division, and I started the new year, 1990, with new people who were eager to be part of a successful business. At the time, we had seven dealers who purchased Texaco products; a few had such small business volume that they eventually closed their accounts. Texaco discouraged us from diversifying our supply chain, but I knew we needed to find another supplier. Through my contacts, I learned Exxon was interested in supplying our area. My staff was worried, given the recent Exxon Valdez accident in Alaska, but I pushed forward, saying, "Let's try it anyway."

Even though I once dreaded talking with people on the

phone, I made a cold call to Exxon's vice president to discuss the possibility of Exxon being our supplier. We spoke at length about how our part of the market could be best served, and I used every skill I had to negotiate a good deal with Exxon. Soon after that call, we signed a supplier contract and began to bring in new clients. Giving clients a choice of products turned out to be exactly what our business model needed. Even though Texaco had threatened to cancel its contract, it remained a supplier alongside Exxon.

We grew the business over the next ten years with consistent telemarketing efforts and sales calls for the commercial fueling department. I served as the general manager until 2000, when I stepped down. I believe the access control business and commercial fueling business' successes were my greatest career achievements.

"Make the most of yourself by fanning the tiny, inner sparks of possibility into flames of achievement."

— Golda Meir

CHAPTER 8

A SECOND CHANCE AT LOVE

"There is no charm equal to tenderness of heart."

— Jane Austen

A s successfully as my career developed after I left California, I wasn't sure I'd find love after my disastrous first marriage. I gained friends after overcoming my fear of speaking through the Dale Carnegie course. I found respect from my colleagues at both the access control business and as a general manager of the commercial fueling business. Yet it still took more nerve than I often had to date, let alone find someone I thought would be my romantic companion for the second half of my life. My perseverance had served me well, though, so I was determined to find love.

After I took the Dale Carnegie course and started the alarm business in Seattle, I dated frequently, but I only ended up getting disappointed and hurt. I was generally attracted to the "elusives," the ones who didn't call after the first date, who belittled me, or who took no interest in me. Even though I'd conquered my disfluency, I had a weight problem, and I tried to hide my intelligence to be more attractive to the men I met. I did anything I thought might catch a man's attention and endear me to him. At singles bars, I'd sip my Scotch and water, sometimes by myself and sometimes with other female friends who were also looking for dates, watching the crowd hopeful for a connection. I was thrilled if a man came up to me and asked me to dance. I found myself attracted to men with reserved personalities because I liked their mystery. I thought my amiable personality would loosen them up and change them into men who could enjoy life with me.

Describe a time you thought changing yourself
would change another person.

What are the drawbacks of this approach?

_____

_____

_____

_____

_____

_____

_____

_____

_____

_____

_____

_____

_____

_____

_____

_____

_____

Even though I endured years of bad dates and rejection, I continued to search for a soul mate. I believed he was out there somewhere, and I believed he would be a completion of me. Maybe that old stigma of being an old maid still haunted me. *People who are thirty* (like me at the time) *should be married*, I thought. Despite my determination, I became so disillusioned with men and the idea of finding my soul mate that I gave up the search by the time I was thirty-four. I focused more strongly on my business because I wanted to feel success someplace in my life. I also thought the more successful I became, the more attractive I would be to men worthy of my attention. Even though I still held to my motto "There must be some way," little did I know that live jazz would be my way to finding love.

Jazz was the soundtrack to my childhood; the music of Duke Ellington, Ella Fitzgerald, Sarah Vaughn, and Count Basie had filled our home. I grew up during the big band jazz era. My dad loved listening to trombone greats like Jack Teagarden, the father of jazz trombone, who also sang with a rich, growly Southern blues voice. My dad was a trombone player who refused to play anything but jazz. Dad's record collection was only jazz. Jazz lifted my spirits and made me want to dance. Whenever I found myself at home alone as a child, I'd lift the lid to the big console record player in our living room, slip a record on the spindle, and gently fit the needle to the groove near the record's edge so it didn't scratch the vinyl. I'd dance around the living room and forget about my disfluency. All that mattered was the music and how wonderful it made me feel. In grade school, I learned to play saxophone since my dad thought the trombone was a man's instrument. I performed in school marching and concert bands throughout middle school, high school, and college. I wanted to sing like Ella Fitzgerald, but my family told me I couldn't hold a tune, and I believed them for a long time.

What arts inspired you as a child? What arts do you wish you had pursued?

_____

_____

_____

_____

When I returned to Washington in 1976 to start my new life, I settled into a new job in Seattle, eighty miles from my parents' home. As I had little social life in Seattle, I would return to Shelton each weekend. Each Saturday night, we would go to the Tumwater Conservatory, which had fine food and live jazz.

My father and mother both had musical backgrounds. My mother played violin in high school. As I previously shared, my dad had been a jazz trombonist from school into his early adult life, when he played professionally. Mom and Dad would travel to Seattle and Portland to hear live jazz. So you can imagine their delight in having quality jazz just twenty miles from home.

The building was previously The Oregon Trail Restaurant and Bar, but the new owners had reimagined the space as a jazz club. The building had three areas inside. At the entrance, a dining room seated forty to fifty people and connected to a small bar with a few stools. The nightclub occupied the area nearest the highway. It had small tables with seating for about fifty. A small stage covered one wall of the nightclub and could comfortably accommodate a band. On St. Patrick's Day, the stage was often filled to capacity with an eighteen-person band performing.

The place was run by Red Kelly, a bass player, and his wife Donna, who did the cooking. The food was four to five-star dining—steaks, specials, seafood—even corned beef and cabbage, especially on St. Patrick's Day. Folks from all over the Olympia area came for the good food and even better music. Members of trios from throughout the Puget Sound area played at the Tumwater Conservatory as guests of The Red Kelly Jazz Trio. Bill Ramsey from Tacoma played saxophone, Freddy Greenwell from Seattle played saxophone, and Ernestine Anderson from Seattle often sang.

Red had played with both big band and jazz bands over the decades, including the popular Harry James and his orchestra. Later, in the '70s, he formed The Red Kelly Jazz Trio with friends. Patrons loved Red's comedy and the music he played six nights a week. Since The Oregon Trail was located so close to the state capital, the bar attracted an odd array of jazz aficionados, politicians, and reporters. In 1976, during an after-hours party, a patron suggested Red run for state office. A local reporter sent a piece to the wire service, proclaiming Red would run for state governor as a member of the OWL party. At one point, OWL stood for "Out With Logic" while other times it stood for "On With Lunacy." The biographies of OWL party members, all drawn from Red's close friends, were so well-written they were included in the official voter's pamphlet that year. In the end, OWL garnered 2 percent of the vote in the general election, a feat unheard of then or since. Around the same time, Jack Perciful, a jazz pianist with the Harry

James Orchestra, joined The Red Kelly Jazz Trio. Jack also joined the OWL party and ran for state treasurer. I would see Jack occasionally on the weekends at the bar, and I was impressed by his musical abilities. Then on July 4, 1984, I met Jack in person at a party my parents hosted.

If you were able to meet someone famous whom you admired, what would you want them to teach you? What would you want them to notice about you?

_____

_____

_____

_____

_____

_____

_____

_____

_____

_____

I recognized Jack not only because he also lived in Olympia, but because he was one of the most sought-after jazz pianists of his time. Jack joined the Harry James Orchestra after other jazz musicians in Los Angeles recommended him to Harry, who then asked him to audition. Jack couldn't afford to travel without being paid, though, so he sent them a taped performance. After hearing his demo tape, the Harry James Orchestra hired him on the spot. His appearance was supposed to be a one-time gig to fill in for an ailing pianist, but Harry had other plans.

"By the way, Jack," Harry said after the show. "We're recording an album at Capitol Records tonight at 6 p.m., so be there a half hour early. Then tomorrow, we leave on a six-week road trip."

Jack enjoyed a long career as a jazz pianist with the Harry James Orchestra until he decided to retire from traveling, and settled in Olympia.

Jack's musical ability interested me first; he played the piano so beautifully that I just melted when I heard him. At the party, as we sat and talked, I found myself drawn to his Irish looks—dark eyes and dark hair. He was kind and quiet, but also very funny.

With his natural charm and ability to read an audience, he knew how to draw people into the music with a touch of the keys.

After the night we met, Jack asked me out to dinner at Lafernos, an Italian restaurant in Seattle. Three musicians were playing that night, and he had known them all thirty years prior to his stint on the Harry James Orchestra. On bass was Buddy Cattlett, a classmate of Quincy Jones, who had also played bass with Count Basie and Louis Armstrong. Andre Thomas played drums, and Lou Rivera played the piano.

After a few songs, Lou asked Jack if he wanted to sit in on the set. Jack willingly took the stage with a smile. He played "There'll Never Be Another You," and it became my song for Jack.

Even though I was still living in the Seattle area and Jack was working in Olympia, we kept in close touch. He called me every night long distance and I'd visit him over the weekends. Over time, I could see he was different from all those elusive types I had dated who had disregarded me. Jack made me a priority in his life, so I didn't feel anxious about our relationship, even when we were apart. He wanted to spend time with me, and I never felt like I had to beg for his attention. He respected what I thought and never felt intimidated by who I was or what I accomplished. We shared the same kind of humor and had very little drama to separate us. I also discovered he had a calming influence on me. Jack and my dad were friends from the Tumwater Conservatory; Dad liked to hear the stories the jazz musicians told about their careers. They had a positive relationship separate from me, which gave Jack a place in my family before we were dating.

Describe your emotional support system. Whom can you count on to be there when you feel sad or confused? What qualities do they bring to your relationship?

_____

_____

_____

_____

_____

_____

_____

_____

_____

_____

_____

_____

_____

_____

_____

_____

_____

Early in our relationship, Jack and I both professed that neither of us wanted to be married again. We saw each other every weekend or so for the next three years, always saying we would not get married. I told him about Kevin and his schemes, and he told me about his previous marriage. He had helped his previous wife raise her two children, then later her four grandchildren. The noisy activity of so many children was hard on his quiet, private nature, and marriage left a bad taste in his mouth since the relationship ended poorly. Even though I was deeply attracted to Jack, I did not want to risk losing him by saying I wanted to marry him. We had become best friends, and I thought that was how our relationship would always be.

Then on my fortieth birthday, Jack presented me with his mother's diamond ring. She had passed away earlier that spring. He gave me a white gold chain to match the band in case I wanted to wear the ring as a necklace. It was like we were teenagers in love. Jack told me his parents had been too poor to afford a wedding ring, so for many years, his mom, Bessie, went without. Then she and her sister started sorting peas in a Moscow, Idaho, pea factory. Her sister didn't have a wedding ring either, so they used a portion of their salaries to buy rings for themselves.

"They were determined women," Jack told me. "Just like you."

I looked at the ring and chain nestled in the palm of my hand, my heart beating fast.

"What does this mean, Jack?"

"It means whatever you want it to mean."

Even in my happiness, I was confused, so I doggedly continued to ask what the ring meant for the next three days. Each time, he gave me the same answer.

"Whatsoever you want it to mean."

On July 3, Jack and I were sitting at the bar at Red Kelly's waiting for him to go on stage. Dad and Mom had once again planned a Fourth of July picnic for the musicians and families the next day. Mom, Dad, and I planned on attending together, but I still wasn't sure whether to wear the ring on my finger.

"We're going to need to figure out what this ring means right now, Jack," I told him that night.

Looking back, it's unclear who proposed, Jack or me. I feel like he vaguely proposed, and I vaguely accepted. We loved each other, even though we were still hesitant about being married.

The next day, one of the musicians at the party asked, "Jack, when are you going to get married?"

Jack laughed and waved a hand dismissively. "Being engaged is bad enough!"

Describe a time when you felt happy. What three components made up that situation and how might you create that situation again?

_____

_____

_____

_____

_____

_____

_____

_____

_____

_____

_____

_____

_____

_____

_____

_____

_____

_____

_____

Exactly a year later, on a Sunday so the musicians could attend, we gathered about 100 of our friends and family together and finally tied the knot. We held the ceremony in the sunken garden at my parents' house. I still remember the heady scent of the late blooming roses. The guests were seated in folding chairs at the base of the garden. The photographer was the same one who had taken my childhood school photos. I wore a light mint dress my sister, Patty Jo, had made for me. Jack wore a mint blazer and pants to match, and a mint and pink striped tie, his nod to formality, since he never wore ties unless he was performing. At the bottom of the garden was a small lake, and at the center of the lake was an island where Supreme Court Justice Robert Utter officiated over the ceremony. Getting someone of Judge Utter's stature was easy; he was a big fan of Jack and his music.

As I stood at the top of the hill waiting for the first chords of "Here Comes the Bride" on the electric piano, I remember thinking that even though Jack was twenty years older than I, if we had twenty years together, we would still have a beautiful life. I crossed a small bridge to the island, and we said our simple vows as our family and friends looked on.

We bought a house behind the Lacey post office. After four years, our home's value doubled, so we sold it and bought a house on the Henderson Inlet, since we both loved the water. Our living room overlooked shellfish beds, and herons and eagles were our neighbors. We designed the room downstairs so Jack could see the water while he practiced on the piano.

For the next twenty years, Jack toured occasionally with the Harry James Ghost Band, created by another Harry James member. He also traveled to festivals with a Dixieland band during the summer. He called me every night when he was away, unless he had to board a ship. We had love, trust, and companionship, and I always knew he would come home to me. I treasured our time together as the second chance at love I knew it to be.

In 2000, Jack contracted Parkinson's and began deteriorating, especially when dementia began to manifest. Soon he could no longer drive, and he suffered a stroke and pneumonia. Still, jazz music was in his blood; his friend, Joe Baque, would bring over an electronic keyboard to play with Jack, and after a set, Jack's walking improved. Whenever he was near a piano, Jack would play, and I could see how happy it made him. On my birthday, he blew me away by playing two songs for me. Still, each day became more and more of a struggle.

"I'm not going to play anymore," he said one day in November 2007. "I'm just embarrassing myself."

The following March, Jack died at the age of eighty-three, having suffered the ravages of Parkinson's for eight years. Even though I went from lover to caregiver, I will never regret the twenty-four years of love we shared. Jack taught me patience—how to wait and not force an outcome. Even though jazz lyrics focus on love—being in love, unrequited love, lost love, somebody to love—Jack also taught me about anger. "Anger is a wasted emotion," he said. He rarely got angry; instead, he put his passion into his music.

"Love is a friendship set to music."

— Joseph Campbell

CHAPTER 9

HOUSE CONCERTS

"Love yourself first and everything else falls into line. You really have to love yourself to get anything done in this world."

— Lucille Ball

For three years, I numbly grieved losing Jack. I was in my mid-sixties, and many of our friends disappeared after his passing. Although sad, losing contact with them was understandable; they were Jack's friends first, then mine. They moved on with their lives while I did my best to adjust to a life without Jack. The only constants in my life were my house, my siblings, and my dog, Rickee.

I had retired by then, too, and I didn't know what to make of the new world in which I found myself. I was faced once again with a new challenge and did my best to see it all as an *adversitunity* just like I'd learned early on. Red Kelly had closed the Tumwater Conservatory in 1978, but up until Jack's passing, I had many other places to enjoy jazz music.

Jack and I often took my parents to jazz festivals within driving distance of our home. The Otter Crest Jazz Festival was held in April on the Oregon coast just a few miles north of Depoe Bay and Newport, Oregon. Back when we attended, the festivals were called jazz parties, and the festival started on a Thursday night and ended on Sunday morning with a blues-gospel service. People rented condos overlooking the shoreline and the concerts were held in a hall that could accommodate 250 people. We were all jazz aficionados and enjoyed set after set with the audience reverently listening without making a sound. Between sets, we'd walk the beach where otters gave birth.

Jim Brown and his wife, Mary, devoted twenty years to organizing the festival. I often wondered if I could organize a jazz festival, but I just as quickly discounted the idea. The time and effort required to gather 100 musicians to perform for an audience of 250 over the course of a weekend was too massive for even my optimistic brain, so I soon forgot the idea.

Have you ever had a *big idea* you thought was

too big for you to handle?

What was your big idea, and what kept you

from following through?

_____

_____

_____

_____

_____

_____

_____

_____

_____

_____

_____

_____

_____

_____

_____

Finally, after three years of grieving, I could think about all the good times Jack and I had shared. Our mutual love for jazz brought us together, and I felt jazz taught me many things about life. For one, it taught me another way of thinking—classical music is very structured, while jazz focuses on improvisation. I can look at problems differently because I feel confident there is always *another way* to achieve my goals, even if I can't see the steps right away. In jazz, musicians take a standard tune and bring in alternate chords, phrasings, and tempos to make each performance unique yet familiar. Before I retired, I could apply lessons learned to solve a current problem, using improvisation to make better, more effective decisions. Jazz made me more comfortable thinking outside of the box to find unusual solutions. As I practiced, my problem-solving skills improved, and I could teach others how to improve theirs as well.

Jazz also emphasizes harmony and cooperation. Musicians collaborate creatively to evoke deep feelings otherwise difficult to access. The audience might focus its attention just on what the soloist is playing, but the entire band listens carefully to the soloist and shifts its performance to support the emerging music. Band members also smoothly and graciously step aside to give other members the spotlight.

Generally, solos can never be repeated because musicians create them on the fly through unstructured, free-flowing improvisation. Established band members can create a kind of stability that allows guests and new performers the space to perform well. The music and performance create a language all members tap into and expand, giving audiences an experience never seen or heard before or after. This exchange of energy creates a pervading sense of optimism, hope, and security that enlivens the listener and performer.

Most of all, jazz taught me to feel joy because the musicians were often humorous and witty, bantering with each other throughout their sets. This sense of play energized me and helped me build a sense of trust even when I did not know where the music would take me next.

Familiar tunes became new again in the hands of a master jazz performer. I loved listening to Jack start a complicated riff on the piano, never knowing where his fingers would take me, following his incredible mind and heart with each trill, pause, and flourish. Behind him, the band would emphasize his riff, play off it, and let it challenge them to do more with their performances than they may have imagined. His art was mysterious, and I could never anticipate how he would resolve each riff.

Being around so many jazz greats, I learned to value good teams whose members support each other's ideas in an effort to create something new.

Jazz is an art of the moment, and I see *adversitunity* as the same: taking a problem and creating an opportunity never imagined before.

What did you learn from my story about jazz (creativity, teamwork, trust, and playfulness)?

Have you applied that lesson before? If so, how? If not, why?

_____

_____

_____

_____

_____

_____

_____

_____

_____

_____

_____

_____

_____

_____

_____

Even though I loved jazz deeply, I waited four years after Jack passed before I experienced live music in our home again. In October 2012, I invited some of Jack's friends and fellow musicians over for a Sunday afternoon party. As the party went on, the musicians wandered downstairs to the basement—Jack's Place, where he used to rehearse at his six-foot-long, Yamaha grand piano. I was upstairs chatting with other guests when I heard the music start. It was no surprise. The musicians had brought their horns—jamming came naturally to them. Soon the other guests followed them downstairs and found seats.

All the musicians had performed with Jack, but not at the same time. They chose some standard jazz tunes like "Giant Steps" by Miles Davis, "Two of Us" by Australian musician David Lewis Luong, Duke Ellington's "Take the 'A' Train," and Count Basie's "April in Paris." It felt just like being at Red Kelly's in 1976, with musicians taking turns with solos. Their playing brought so much joy to my heart that I requested "We'll Be Together Again" as the finale.

My friend Susan Patrick and I sat bobbing our heads and tapping our toes, thoroughly enjoying ourselves. I had met Susan about a decade before and thought right away we would be good friends. Susan and I are the same height, but she is slighter in build, with short blond hair. She is a tenacious and dedicated woman who worked as a state lawyer for several years and created GET, Washington State's guaranteed education tuition program to help parents save for their children's college needs. Even though we only saw each other every three or four years for lunch, we always reconnected as if no time had passed. Susan loved jazz, too, and attended a jazz camp in California every year where she studied with many of the greats, honing her piano skills.

As the applause died down after a song, Susan and I turned to each other and said, "We could have a concert down here," then laughed about how we came up with the same idea for a house concert at the same time.

After the exciting afternoon of listening to musicians jamming in Jack's Place, Susan and I decided we wanted to keep alive the legacy of jazz musicians who had passed, and to support those establishing their careers by hosting house concerts.

Who has helped you in the past and inspires you today?

_____

_____

_____

_____

_____

I learned a house concert is literally a concert in a private home's living room, basement, or even backyard. House concerts have become quite popular in recent years all across the country, with artists performing before audiences of twenty-five to fifty people—groups small enough to fit comfortably in a living room. Both the audience and artist experience an intimacy they would not normally get in a formal concert hall.

Even though house concerts take place in a home, they are concerts in a "listening room" rather than a party with background music. House concerts are different from anything I have ever experienced at a club or bar.

Artists enjoy doing house concerts because, typically, there isn't any smoke, very little or no alcohol with which to compete, little advertising needed, and ticket prices can be whatever the artist and host agree upon.

Audience members enjoy the concerts because they can ask questions about how songs were composed or how instruments are played. The important thing for hosting a house concert is a comfortable space and inviting friends, neighbors, coworkers, or family to attend. The event could be just a concert, or a host could include appetizers and drinks or have a potluck. The options are really wide open.

Even though we were excited to start planning, the holidays followed, so we didn't have time to figure out how to create a regular series of house concerts. Then the following February, Susan called me. Her friend, Ivy, from Jazz Camp, was hosting pianist Overton Berry.

"I've got two tickets to her house concert in West Seattle," she said. "Want to join me?"

Ivy had been organizing house concerts for a few years, so I quickly accepted the invitation. I was anxious to experience my first house concert, something deliberately planned rather than spontaneous.

On a Saturday night, Susan and I headed north to enjoy a wonderful evening of music with fifty other patrons. We were a diverse group, old and young, smartly dressed and casual. Our tickets came with a single glass of wine and three appetizers. We milled around the narrow room, sipping and munching before the show began. Chairs were arranged three on each side with an aisle down the middle that led to a piano and wide space where the musicians played.

Susan and I settled in the best seats we could find. Student vocalists from Jazz Camp performed first, and soon we were all clapping and laughing, our heads bobbing to the beat.

Then Overton Berry settled onto the piano bench and started us on a musical journey reminiscent of all my years with Jack.

Overton has his own style, though. I was happy to be back in such a familiar space with others who appreciated the music as much as I do.

The evening was full of laughter and joy, and I was glad I had gone with Susan to the concert.

"We could do it, Kathy," said Susan as we traveled back to Olympia. "We could have our own series of house concerts in Jack's Place!"

"Yes," I said, my mind already planning the details. "We can plan them based on the concert we just saw. I know we can do it. I know we *will* do it!"

The next day, we strategized over the phone and came up with the name "Swingin' Sounds" for our house concert series. As luck would have it, the matching domain name was available through the GoDaddy webhosting service. Susan created the website and ordered business cards that same day.

"Kathy," said Susan, "we're going to need chairs and dishes for the concert. Where are we going to get the money for that?"

"Jack's piano will need tuning too," I replied. I paused, thinking about our dilemma. "Let me call you back, Susan. I have an idea."

After I hung up, I started searching my office. I remembered seeing a check for Jack's life insurance policy in my files. Once I found it, I was surprised by the amount: $1,000. The check was three years old, and I was afraid it might not be valid. I called Susan back and told her what I'd found.

"The check is old, but I think it's a sign from Jack," I said. The next day, we promptly headed to the bank and smoothly made a deposit, seed money for our concert series. I knew in my heart that Jack approved of our venture.

Since Susan is more knowledgeable about contemporary jazz musicians than I am, she became our connection to the performers for our concerts. She called the artists to check their availability over the next few months. We even called Ivy, who mentored us via Skype, giving us tips on organization and promotion. There was so much interest that by the following Thursday, we had our first concert scheduled—it would be in April with another scheduled for June.

Our first performer in 2013 was Shanna Carlson, a vocalist and pianist from California and an instructor at Jazz Camp. Shanna writes her own material and is very accomplished in creating moods with her music: romantic, playful, sometimes introspective. She brought the delightful Argentinian guitar player Hugo Wainzinger and the renowned Brazilian jazz piano player Jovino Santos Neto with her.

We set the concert time for two in the afternoon and planned for an audience of thirty, drawn from our circle of friends and family, who were willing to pay the $25 ticket price to cover the cost of the performers. We served wine and appetizers and mingled and chatted for a half hour while we enjoyed the view over the inlet. Herons flew overhead while the waves gently touched the beach below. We created an intimate, comfortable setting everyone enjoyed.

Eventually, we all meandered downstairs where Jack's piano, newly tuned, took center stage. On the walls were memorabilia from Jack's career, and I could feel him very close, knowing he would have enjoyed the performance.

Shanna, with her red pixie-cut and long, flowing gown, sang first and brought a personable energy to the concert that was both vibrant and comfortable. Her smoky voice filled the room with emotion I could feel in my chest. Hugo's guitar stylings came next, then Jovino played on Jack's piano, his fingers creating complex and rich music that beautifully reflected his Brazilian heritage.

The concert was very informal, with conversations between the audience and performers throughout. We were mesmerized by the musician's skill, and we laughed at each other's jokes. Outside, the day turned rainy, but we didn't care—we were enjoying each other's company.

Before the second set, we took a twenty-minute break to enjoy dessert and more wine. The performers felt appreciated and welcomed, enjoying the chance to connect with each other, too, since they didn't normally tour together.

By the time the second set was done an hour later, Susan and I knew we had created something very special: a place that would become a favored venue in the future. We knew we could bring together the right combination of performers, audience, and atmosphere, and bring a magical experience to everyone.

We went on providing a comfortable, intimate setting for performers to share their music with small, attentive audiences for the next six years. Jazz styles included mainstream, Cuban, and Brazilian. We hosted Grammy Award nominees like Randy Porter, Pete Christlieb, and Josh Turner. Vocalist Ed Reed, a *Downbeat* magazine Rising Star (at age eighty-five) from San Francisco, and Gail Pettis, a prominent Seattle vocalist featured in *Oprah* magazine, also performed for us. Willi Bays, a local sixteen-year-old saxophone player who traveled with the Monterey Jazz Festival, also performed. We featured Bill Ramsey, an eighty-nine-year-old baritone sax player who performed with my own father at the Evergreen Ballroom and later with Count Basie, and Joe Baque, a ninety-two-year-old piano player originally from New York.

In addition to Washington, musicians came from California, Colorado, Oregon, and British Columbia to play our concerts. The musicians often asked if they could take our patrons on the road with them because they had such a positive experience playing the Swingin' Sounds concert series. Over the next five years, over 150 musicians have performed and nearly 1,000 audience members have witnessed the magic that can occur at our concerts. The series continues to be a joy for Susan and me because it's a way we can support the extraordinary musicians of the Northwest and beyond while watching our friends enjoy these special events.

Describe an experience that seemed improbable, yet, when you worked toward it, your vision became a reality:

_____

_____

_____

_____

_____

_____

_____

_____

_____

_____

_____

_____

_____

_____

_____

_____

Creating Swingin' Sounds taught Susan and me many skills and brought us resources that supported the development of enjoyable and sustainable community events. Among the lessons we learned are:

Teamwork—We divided up tasks based on our personal desires and talents. Susan knew musicians on the West Coast and became the main contact point for hiring and scheduling talent. She also has kept the webpage (https://www.swingin-sounds.com) up to date. I took up the administrative duties, such as sending out notices for upcoming events, taking reservations, and buying beverages.

Over time, people offered to volunteer, and we accepted their help willingly and gratefully. Currently, we have volunteers who make appetizers, take the entrance fees, post event notices on Facebook.

Keep it simple—Susan and I focused on our audience—they were attending primarily to enjoy the music. We wanted the venue to feel comfortable and welcoming, and having food and drink was a nice touch, but we didn't worry about fancy stage lighting or expensive advertising.

Communication in service to goals—Susan and I discussed issues together as they came up, like musician cancellations or lack of audience, and talked through the process of producing and promoting shows before, during, and after each performance, to identify where we could improve things in the future.

Enjoy the moment—On those fluke evenings when 20 percent of our audience didn't show up, Susan and I decided not to worry and focused instead on who was there and the musicians we had invited. By relieving ourselves of this anxiety, we made our evenings fun for ourselves and our audience.

Intimate settings foster community—The intimate setting we created for Swingin' Sounds fosters a sense of family where audience members feel comfortable asking the musicians questions they wouldn't normally ask at a concert. Musicians share stories about how songs were created and how instruments work. The distance between audience and musician disappears, leaving a real sense of camaraderie and joy.

Take breaks—Audience members can become as fatigued as performers, so we discovered that including breaks helped everyone stay comfortable and at ease. The breaks also gave musicians a chance to connect with each other.

Importance of building each other up—Susan and I built a level of trust that allows us to take over for each other whenever one of us suffers a personal setback. When Susan fell down the stairs, I took over the show's correspondence and bookings. When I was sick, Susan took over the more routine tasks to ensure we had food and drink available for shows. We recently added a third member to our team, Stacy Sharp, who provides appetizers and beverages.

Keeping the vision—Throughout the development of the Swingin' Sounds concert series, we kept in sight the idea of honoring the legacy of legendary musicians and their contributions to jazz. We encouraged musicians to play what they wanted: originals, selections from their latest albums, or classics they found significant to their development.

"I'm always thinking about creating…. Every day
I find something creative to do with my life."

— Miles Davis

CHAPTER 10

TOASTMASTERS CONTESTS

"When the whole world is silent, even

one voice becomes powerful."

— Malala Yousafzai

If my love of jazz became the Swingin' Sounds concert series, then joining Toastmasters International in 2009 helped the little two-year old who loved performing on her grandparents' stone hearth to reemerge. Since 1924, Toastmasters has taught its members public speaking and leadership skills through a worldwide network of clubs. I found Capitol Club by visiting Toasmasters' website.

In 2009, I had been widowed for a year and a half, and the

life I had known for the previous twenty-four was over. I was looking for a new start when a friend suggested Toastmasters. Capitol Club was nearby, held meetings on Tuesday evenings, and fit with my schedule. Even so, I entered the meeting room with some apprehension. Who was I going to meet? Would they like me? Was Toastmasters something I wanted to become involved with?

As I tried to get my bearings, I was greeted by a warm, friendly woman, stylishly dressed in a black pantsuit. "Hi. I'm Angela," she said. "You can sign in as a guest over here; then you can come sit by me." I followed her directions and felt welcome immediately.

As we settled in our seats, Angela explained how Capitol Club ran and told me about some of the members. Another member, Roselie, sat nearby and chimed in about all of the awards the club had won and the award-winning speakers who were members. It made me feel motivated to learn more.

The meeting was a blur to me, even though my new friend Angela patiently explained the events as they occurred. I know the club left a favorable impression on me because I was ready to join by the end of the meeting. Members approached me after the meeting, too, and gave me their contact information in case I had any questions. Their friendly openness sealed the deal for me, and I looked forward to seeing them the following week.

Since joining Capitol Club, I have increased my communication and leadership skills and, as a side benefit, I made a circle of friends that continues to grow.

We met regularly in a narrow meeting room with just enough space to seat about sixteen people at a restaurant called the Urban Onion.

My confidence grew, and I started giving speeches a few weeks after joining. Standing in front of a dozen or so people and delivering my ideas with a skill I had only imagined in years past delighted me. They appreciated my speeches, and I enjoyed being the center of attention, just as I had as a child.

What groups do your friends belong to that interest you?

How might these groups fit with your vision of your best life?

_____

_____

_____

_____

_____

_____

_____

_____

_____

_____

_____

_____

_____

_____

_____

_____

_____

_____

Toastmasters training is more open-ended than the Dale Carnegie Institute, which focused primarily on developing confidence and a fixed length for speeches. The structure of Toastmasters allows for refined speeches by emphasizing that good speeches have a beginning, middle, and end. We learned many different skills for delivering good speeches, like varying speech patterns, incorporating movements and gestures, and using personal stories to emphasize concepts and themes. Over time, we learned ten different kinds of speeches, culminating in giving an inspirational speech.

Many people look to food for comfort, and there is plenty of it at Toastmasters events. Members jokingly "whine" and dine together as they offer constructive feedback. They trade contacts, techniques, and resources. They train and work together, and they cry and cheer together.

Working closely on projects at Toastmasters brought out the best in me. In early 2015, I competed to deliver a speech at the International Toastmasters Conference in Las Vegas, Nevada. The top 100 speakers compete to become the world's best speaker. I decided to create an inspirational speech based on overcoming stuttering.

Contests were led by a Master of Ceremonies, and an Evaluator gave points based on how well we used the skills we had learned and deducted points for excessive pauses and using "um" and "ah."

I felt anxious before my first contest. I wanted to win so badly that I practiced my speech nightly in front of friends or on my own. I felt relieved when I won at the Club level, but I still had more levels to win the following week.

A couple of the Toastmasters members offered to help me improve my speech. One videotaped me speaking so I could see how I actually looked, and the other helped me work on my content.

I went on to win at the area and division levels, each time feeling more confident about my accomplishments. Finally, I competed at the district level, and although I did not win, I felt accomplished placing third. After all, who would have thought a stutterer would win a speech contest in front of dozens of people?

In addition to education, experience, inspiration, team building, and leadership opportunities, Toastmasters fosters strong friendships. Every club has members who are going through a crisis or have overcome an extreme challenge. Deadlines, let alone tragedies, draw people together who might not otherwise associate. By sharing our experiences, we learn from each other and become more confident wherever we are in our lives. Members create families as they expand their social connection beyond club meetings; some of my most valued friendships were seeded in Toastmasters.

One friend, Daryl Murrow, introduced me to my vocation as a business mentor. Another Toastmasters friend, Margi, rented my apartment, and Angela hosted holiday dinners for us single folks. I have friends on whom I can call for impromptu dinners or necessary trips to the hospital, and these friendships have supported me as a retired single woman as I've grown older.

What values do you need to see reflected in the groups you are involved with?

_____

_____

_____

_____

_____

_____

_____

_____

_____

_____

_____

_____

_____

_____

_____

_____

_____

_____

Early in my first year in Toastmasters, Daryl and I discovered a mutual passion—business ownership! He was developing his business coaching career and was interested in my stories of building and maintaining a successful business. I was honored to assist him however I could, and soon, he became my business co-conspirator and a dear friend.

At the same time, a group of ten Toastmaster women came together and formed a sisterhood known as the "Ya-Yas" after the bestselling novel *The Divine Secrets of the Ya-Ya Sisterhood* by Rebecca Wells. Like the four friends in the novel, we Ya-Yas developed a sisterly bond and helped each other overcome many challenges. At any given time, there are about a dozen Ya-Yas, a group of single and married, professional women. We range in age from fifty to sixty; I'm the oldest, now at seventy-three. One Ya-Ya is an author, while others are doctors, schoolteachers, state employees, or retired.

Over the years, we've come to rely on each other. We each know that when we need help, the Ya-Yas are there, whether it's a ride from the airport, a medical appointment, or a much appreciated conversation. None of us hesitate to help, and there are plenty of us to response quickly to personal needs despite our busy schedules. We also have fun together enjoying holiday dinners at Angela's home, birthday celebrations, hiking, boating, and impromptu get-togethers on Friday nights at a local restaurant.

With the Ya-Yas and the Toastmasters, I felt wanted and like I belonged once again. I cared deeply about these people and knew they cared about me.

Then Bobbi, one of the Ya-Yas, invited me to attend a program she was presenting at a local Rotary Club. She explained that Rotary International is a group of service-minded professionals who lend their talents to support projects both locally and internationally. Having been a business person for more than twenty-five years, I couldn't believe I hadn't known much about Rotary before. At best, I thought it was a men's club. Now I was intrigued to learn more.

The day of Bobbi's presentation, I found my way to one of Olympia's marinas. Below the marina's popular restaurant was the Viewpoint Room where the local Rotary Club met. As I entered, I spotted a woman serving as a cashier at the door. After handing her my lunch fee, I realized my belief that Rotary was just for men had just been cheerfully debunked.

"Hi, Kathy," Bobbi greeted me as I came through the door. "The buffet is this way." She led me to a series of long tables against the far wall, and we fell into line. Salad greens and dressings came first, then a vegetable medley of broccoli and squashes. The main entrée of turkey, mashed potatoes, and gravy came next, followed by a table loaded with three different kinds of cookies.

I followed Bobbi as she found us seats at one of the round tables. There was enough seating for about eighty people, and she steered me to a table where two of her friends, both attorneys, sat. I feel uneasy around people in the legal profession because of a long-held belief that they are adversarial by nature. I don't like this because I can be verbally clubbed in any conversation, unable to hold my own on any topic.

To my surprise, both attorneys had a good sense of humor that matched my own. A lively twenty-minute conversation ensued and yet another faulty belief disappeared. I glanced around the room and saw other lively conversations filled with laughter were going on.

Soon after we finished our meal, a bell rang and the meeting began. Under the club president's careful direction, the meeting ran smoothly from saluting the flag and offering prayers to reciting the four-way test: Is it the truth? Is it fair to all concerned? Will it build goodwill and better friendships? Will it be beneficial to all concerned? Over the next hour or so, I could see how foundational the Rotary motto "Service Above Self" was for the club.

Bobbi's presentation was well received, and the meeting ended promptly at 1:15. As I left the Viewpoint Room, I felt a philanthropic longing reemerge after twenty years. I had set it aside for other projects and people.

Later, I researched the Rotary Club's origins. It was formed by Paul P. Harris in Chicago, Illinois. He gathered three business acquaintances one day in late February 1905, with the vision of sharing knowledge, forming lifelong friendships, and giving back to their communities. Over the following century, Rotary International bloomed into a membership of 1.2 million people in 220 countries and 34,000 clubs. Beginning in 1979, several clubs came together to eradicate polio, a disease that left children crippled and living in machines called Iron Lungs with little hope for a normal life. Through the efforts of Rotary members, six million vaccinations were purchased and sent to the Philippines for a multi-year project. Although coordinating such a project seemed daunting to other service groups, this partnership between countries and Rotary Clubs expanded, immunizing more than three billion children in 122 countries, and reducing instances of polio by 99.9 percent worldwide.

This story revived my belief in the human spirit and the ability of communities like Rotary International to make extraordinary things happen.

What beliefs lift you up and inspire you to act?

Which communities support you in taking action?

_____

_____

_____

_____

_____

_____

_____

_____

I attended the Rotary lunches regularly, making them a priority in my week. Not only were there members I wanted to get to know better, but there were also outstanding programs focused on our local, regional, and global communities. Sometimes entertaining and other times thought-provoking, the talks gave me perspective on topics I had never considered. With the vision of service above self, we discussed issues such as homelessness, education, local service projects, and global projects, such as clean water and peace through education.

"The best way to find yourself is to lose yourself in the service of others."

— Mahatma Gandhi

CHAPTER 11

GIVING BACK

"It does not matter how slowly you go,

so long as you don't stop."

— Confucius

After being a member of Rotary for about a year, the club asked me to be the membership chair, and I agreed. With only a sketchy outline for instructions, I looked to membership chairs from other clubs for ideas. I learned that each club's approach to attracting and retaining members was different. Some clubs had a lengthy initiation process requiring new members to accomplish as many as twelve tasks prior to becoming a regular member, while another club only required a successful interview with the club president over coffee.

Our club fell in the middle, requiring new members to lead a flag salute and assist the Sergeant at Arms in creating a safe, welcoming space. We also asked potential members to give a classification talk about themselves and their careers, attend an orientation session about the Rotary Club's vision and goals, join a committee within the club, and attend a board meeting. Unafraid of change, and pulling from my years of business ownership and management, I suggested some activities be eliminated to give prospective members a simpler, quicker path to membership. When the board agreed with my suggestions, I knew I was on the right track.

Additionally, club members were under the impression they must attend every meeting—not so. My research found no such requirements from Rotary International. It was up to the individual club to determine whether meetings were mandatory. Once I shared this information with the board, attendance requirements significantly relaxed. Two years later, membership had significantly increased with 20 percent of membership under the age of forty.

What skills and experiences can you offer a service organization or other volunteer agency to support its goals?

_____

_____

_____

_____

_____

_____

_____

_____

_____

_____

_____

_____

_____

_____

_____

_____

_____

The membership chair's responsibilities consisted primarily of administrative tasks around initiating new members. The benefit of being membership chair for me was that it made me feel more comfortable introducing myself and getting to know the other members. Our club remained steady at around sixty members—seven new members joined during the year, and seven members didn't renew at the end of the year. Truthfully, I felt a bit frustrated that my efforts to shepherd new members through the initiation process did not result in growth.

One day, the club was presenting awards to members who had provided leadership and service to the club. It was an enjoyable evening of good food and companionship in a room filled with laughter and conversation, just like my Carnegie experience and my jazz community. Many of my friends received well-deserved awards and applauded enthusiastically as others received honors for their hard work. Between speeches, I chatted with friends at my table, looking up whenever a familiar name was read.

"And now Percykathiful," said the master of ceremonies.

The name was unfamiliar, and I looked around, searching the room for the person.

"Percykathiful?"

Others lifted their heads checking to see who stood up. Still nothing.

"Percykathiful!"

"I think that's you! She's gotten your name twisted around," I heard someone at my table say.

Laughter filled the room, then applause. I stood with a smile and accepted my Foundation Recognition pin.

As I left after the meeting, several called out, "See you next week, Percy!"

The name resonated with me, so much so that I decided to keep it—Perci with an "i" for the feminine spelling.

Later, I Googled "Perci" to see if it was taken. I found a definition for "Perci"—*feminine, yet spunky*. The name was the perfect fit for this new leg of my journey in Rotary. I changed my Rotary badge to "Perci," and I'm now even known outside of Rotary by that name.

In what ways have you celebrated and shown a change in status or identity?

_____

_____

_____

_____

_____

_____

_____

_____

_____

_____

_____

_____

_____

_____

_____

_____

_____

The club presidency opened up two years later, and a search for nominees began. There hadn't been a woman president in a number of years, and the membership hoped a woman would step forward. I considered stepping up to the challenge. The club president led weekly meetings, monthly board meetings, and made decisions big and small during their term. The president also attended meetings outside the club and managed email on behalf of the club. It all seemed so daunting, especially since I had begun to experience some health issues. Ultimately, I felt too old to be president, since I was already in my late sixties.

Then, the club invited legislative candidates running for Washington State Legislature to one of our weekly programs. One of the candidates shared how she had been battling a significant health issue for most of her adult life. She was my age, and yet, even with age and health considerations, she was embracing this next challenge.

I saw myself letting age and health issues hold me back. At that very moment, I decided to step forward as a nominee for club president. The membership accepted my nomination and no one else was interested in the position, so I began my year as president elect and trained to check off another bucket list item: Rotary Club President.

The lessons I have learned as Rotary president have been profound and, in some cases, life changing. The leadership skills I learned during my business ownership years also worked with a volunteer organization—find the right people for the job, set parameters, and get out of their way, checking in occasionally to monitor progress.

I learned to ask others for help, rather than being the Lone Ranger. The members were happy to help in any way, from leading a weekly meeting to helping with paperwork overflow, and I learned to be myself. Occasionally, my sense of humor would appear and was usually well received.

And yet, even with all my activity with Rotary International and the Ya-Yas, I felt restless. In 2012, the year I joined Rotary and initiated the house concerts, I was still struggling with my new status as retiree. I craved some meaningful work, something with a purpose.

"What should I be doing now?" I asked Daryl. At that time,

Daryl was the business resource manager at Thurston County's Economic Development Council (EDC). He was well acquainted with what was going on in the business community.

"You would make an awesome SCORE volunteer," he immediately replied. He went on to explain that the Service Corps of Retired Executives, or SCORE, was a national organization with chapters throughout the country that provided advice and mentoring to small businesses.

"There's an active chapter in Lacey," he said, "and they are looking for experienced retired executives like you to mentor people who want to start a business or who have an issue in their existing business."

How open are you to opportunities and training?

What support do you need to embrace

opportunities for training?

_____

_____

_____

_____

_____

_____

_____

_____

_____

_____

_____

_____

_____

_____

_____

_____

_____

Daryl connected me with Dick Wadley, the head of the Lacey Chapter of SCORE, who explained more about the opportunity.

I did not immediately join, however. I thought I didn't know enough about communicating business practices to others to be of value. I worried about what would happen if I gave the wrong advice; a new business might fail because of me, and I didn't want that to happen.

Dick was persistent, though. He could see something about me that I couldn't see. He continued to contact me, hoping I would join. Finally, I gave in, took the SCORE test, and attended my first mentoring session with Dick as the lead counselor.

As Dick and I learned more about our clients' business needs, I realized I need not have been concerned about having nothing to contribute. Within an hour of taking the SCORE test, I was sharing my experiences with Dick and a client who was developing a start-up business. Dick focused on marketing and finances, such as the costs associated with the start-up. I talked about the importance of support from family and friends, and encouraged the client to be sure everyone was onboard with the idea. After my experiences with my ex-husband and the security systems, I knew every business has an emotional side people often overlook.

What risks have you taken and what solutions have you used that might help less-experienced people succeed?

_____

_____

_____

_____

_____

_____

_____

_____

_____

_____

_____

_____

Business owners' families and friends will likely be affected by the risks the owner is taking. Family and friends are often uncomfortable raising concerns, though, since they want to be supportive. Start-ups are time consuming, and I advised the client to continuously communicate the business' progress to family and friends so they would feel more comfortable. Dick was impressed, and I felt confident in my advisory role. By the end of the consultation, we both knew the training wheels were off, and I could mentor on my own.

Over the next five years, I had the opportunity to share my experiences and knowledge with hundreds of clients at the Thurston County EDC as a SCORE mentor. Working with women, men, and occasionally couples, I reviewed business plans before they were submitted to banks, credit unions, or investors. We tailored the plans to fit each audience, ensuring appeals for support were received positively.

Eager potential business owners asked me if their ideas were viable and, if so, what steps they needed to take next. As I mentored others, I often thought it would have been great to have had a SCORE mentor for some of my startups. With good advice,

I would have passed on a couple of businesses, saving both money and lost sleep.

It felt good to pay my experience forward, helping seasoned yet distraught business owners who thought they had a thriving business but suddenly realized they were out of money. When we met, the business owners often put too much emphasis on gaining clients and completing transactions. I showed them they needed to face the reality of their bottom line. Once they understood they would be out of money or even out of business if they didn't face reality, they got serious about their business' financial side.

I also helped prospective business buyers decide if the companies were good investments and what terms they should request. Usually, I gave my opinion, remaining neutral, knowing it was not ultimately my decision. However, once I pleaded with a couple not to purchase an existing retail clothing store. It had not been profitable for at least three years, and I knew the business had little chance of succeeding. Since they both planned to work there, the store would be their only source of income. It reminded me of selling alarms with my first husband, and although I didn't tell them my own story, I knew what the future might hold for them.

Some consultations required my Encourager Hat. In one case, a woman had the opportunity to purchase the dog-boarding business she had managed for five years. The owners were offering her a sweet deal, and it was apparent to me she should buy the business. She hesitated, though, worried the business would fail. I could tell all she needed was the courage to step into the new role.

"You must buy this business," I said adamantly. "I can see you're passionate about the dogs and their owners. You know the business inside and out! You've managed it on your own for five years already." She took my advice and bought the business. Later, I learned she had gone on to make prudent decisions regarding expenditures, focusing investments on revenue-producing upgrades like additional fencing to accommodate more dogs. After three years, she was thriving and continuing to build the business in realistic stages, only expanding with affordable, revenue-producing services and goods.

How can you encourage others to live their best lives?

_____

_____

_____

_____

_____

_____

_____

_____

_____

_____

_____

_____

_____

_____

_____

_____

_____

Every business and business owner is unique, and I'm grateful for the opportunity to pass on my business experience and knowledge to others free of charge. My mentorship covered not just the subjects traditionally taught in college like marketing, finance, operations, and leadership, but I also shared "soft skills," such as overcoming the fear of success, fear of failure, and fear of having money, and providing alternative viewpoints on traditional business methods.

Working with SCORE was a wonderful experience, one that stretched me personally, mentally, and emotionally. Mentoring kept my brain active and sharpened my listening skills. I always did my best to share my practical experience and provide my clients with valuable insights they could use immediately and in the future.

"When you talk, you give yourself away. You reveal your true character in a picture, which is more true and realistic than anything an artist can do for you."

— Ralph Smedley, founder of Toastmasters

CHAPTER 12

LIVING MY BEST LIFE

"The only person you should strive to be better than is the person you were yesterday."

— Matty Mullins

Skydiving

In 2015, at the age of sixty-eight, I started my "encore life." I decided to take the lessons I'd learned and my experiences and use them to become the best me possible. Still, I never imagined my lessons would take me to the point of jumping out of a perfectly good airplane. Or that my fear of singing in front of others would be overcome by following a few simple steps.

Like many ideas I had throughout my life, skydiving wasn't an impulse decision. As luck would have it, my good friend Daryl decided to face his fear of heights in 2015. Each year, on his birthday, he tackles a long-held fear, and he told our mutual friend, Stephen, that he wanted to try tandem skydiving for his birthday. Stephen thought it was a great idea and invited me to join them, but I was afraid of heights.

I only had two weeks to get over the fear. After several conversations, I discovered two other friends were also facing their fear of heights by skydiving. I was stuck on an early draft of this book, so Stephen thought skydiving might be just the thing to shake my creative process open again.

My training at the Dale Carnegie Institute had taught me to ask myself, "What's the worst thing that could happen?" Once I knew the worst, then I could prepare to accept it and still go forward, improving on the worst.

The two worst things I thought could happen with skydiving were death and dismemberment. I went to the Internet and researched tandem skydiving and its dangers. First, I learned I had more chance of dying on the way to the jump than because of the jump itself. Tandem jumpers are required to complete 500 jumps before jumping with a student, and in Western Washington, there had only been one death from skydiving in recent years. What about being maimed? I watched YouTube videos about jumping for a couple of days. Dismemberment due to bad landings never happened, and watching the videos desensitized me to the fear because I knew more about what to expect.

I've learned that FEAR is an acronym for False Evidence Appearing Real, and that fear simply represents what could go wrong. But I actually had evidence that my fears were based in fact. When I was ten years old, I nearly drowned after diving head first into a body of water. Even though I survived, the fear of what *could* go wrong the next time had developed into a fear of heights. As an adult, driving over high bridges and mountain passes, especially if I could see deep canyons below, made my heart pound. Even though I wanted to face my fear and had done what I could to desensitize myself, I was still afraid of failing, of being hurt, or worst of all, dying.

So why did I entertain the idea of risking my life doing a

free fall for forty-five seconds at a terminal velocity of 120 miles per hour?

When I told my friend Rose Anne about my plans, her eyes bugged out and her jaw dropped.

"That just puts you in crazy-old lady territory!" she said. I had just turned sixty-eight and my fiftieth class reunion was a few days away, so I was super-sensitive to the remark. I didn't want to be an old lady, frail and wondering when her life had passed her by. Rose Anne's remark was the tipping point. FEAR is also an acronym for Face Everything and Rise. Skydiving with my friends would give me the chance to overcome my fear of heights and change my challenge into an *adversitunity.*

The jump was on! I knew it would be a life-changing event. Even with all my fears, I wanted to be part of Daryl and Stephen's group, taking the leap out of that airplane.

On a sunny August Sunday, Wild Bill greeted us at the jump site. A grizzled man in his seventies with khaki shorts and a Crocodile Dundee hat, he claimed to have been a Hollywood stunt man. He kept us entertained with his alleged feats while we waited for the main event. He even claimed that every Wednesday, local skydivers jumped naked together and formed a circle formation as they fell to Earth. He was quite the character and seemed to enjoy his job.

The jump site looked like a homeless encampment with trailers and lean-tos scattered about a large grassy field. Before we boarded the plane, we watched a briefing video of various jumps, all meant to scare the non-committed. No one changed their mind.

Finally, we signed a multi-page document releasing the jump company from any liability. (The video alluded to, "This may be the last video you ever watch.") A little voice of apprehension crept into my mind.

Fitted with parachutes packed by high school girls, we trudged to the waiting plane. After all, as John Wayne said, "Courage is being scared to death and saddling up anyway."

Just before takeoff, I felt like I might back out, so I announced that I wanted to be the first jumper. I wanted to be first so I would be sure to jump.

At 10,500 feet above the ground, I stood in front of Kyle,

my jump master, whose body was strapped to mine for our tandem skydive.

"Kathy!" he yelled over the wind. "Remember to cross your arms over your chest, hold your head back, and arch your back!" My new best friend kept repeating his words, but they didn't stick and it didn't matter. Soon my feet were dangling in the wind and there was nothing to hold onto.

Nothing but blue sky.

Suddenly, Kyle shoved me out of the plane—at my request.

GERONIMO!

We were free falling at 120 miles per hour, hurtling toward the ground. The force of the air against us pulled open my mouth. Photographic evidence would later show just my teeth as I screamed, "I'm going to die!"

Then, with a jolt, our parachute opened, and we began to float, our speed drastically reduced.

"Are you okay?" shouted Kyle into my ear. "I've had men faint on me."

I nodded and gave him a thumbs up, my amazement taking away the words I needed to describe my feelings. As we drifted down, I saw the green and yellow countryside below us and the ocean beyond. In the distance, Mount Rainier sat cloaked in white, while to the south, I saw the torn face of Mount St. Helens.

Above the traffic of the city and away from the noisy plane engines, the air was quiet and warm. I didn't have much time to enjoy the view, though, because soon enough we were landing.

We had been taught to lift up our legs at touchdown, then scoot into the landing on our backsides. As Kyle and I approached the ground, though, my legs instinctively went underneath me, and I landed on my knees—not a pretty landing. I strained a muscle in my right leg that pained me for the rest of the day.

I have a hundred pictures and several minutes of video documenting my successful descent and landing on the grassy field. Later that day, we celebrated together at an upscale bar and restaurant in Toledo, Washington. We shared stories of how it felt to jump, to fall, to land. Our eyes shone with excitement and wonder about it all.

I conquered my lifelong fear of heights that day.

When I returned home, my friend Angela from the Ya-Yas called and invited me to dinner with Jane and Eddie, two other Ya-Yas. As we settled in to eat, I kept my demeanor friendly but cool. Inside, my performer's heart waited for the best moment. Soon everyone was sharing recent stories. Then Angela turned to me.

"What did you do today, KP?" she asked.

I waited a beat, then shrugged.

"I jumped out of a plane," I replied, then took a bite of my food.

The table went silent, and no one moved except to stare at me. I felt the corner of my mouth lift as the delight at shocking my friends took hold.

"You *what*?" exclaimed Jane.

"When? How?" sputtered Eddie.

I shrugged again, then leaned back in my chair, letting my story of survival unfold. I may have embellished it a bit, but only like any good jazz artist improvising for the sake of the audience's enjoyment.

"That's amazing, KP!" said Angela. We laughed at how overcoming fears can be so challenging and yet so rewarding.

Knowing what we want, and what we don't want, allows us to stay focused on pursuing our goals. Even though facing our fears is almost always the last thing we want to do, it is what we need to do most.

If you want it badly enough, you can make it happen. Hope helps us unlearn the patterns we create through fear. Hope shifts our focus toward the future by allowing us to see a difficult past can make a successful future even more rewarding.

In my encore life, I used the eight key elements for creating *adversitunities* to create a new vision for my best life.

1. Detailed Goal Statement—Go skydiving.

2. List of Skills and Resources—Watch YouTube videos. Find trustworthy skydiving company.

3. Allies—Daryl and Stephen.

4. Expert—Kyle, Jump Master.

5. Vision of Future Self—Someone brave enough to jump out of a plane.

6. Specific Goal Date—The week before my fiftieth class reunion.

7. Supporting Others—Daryl and Stephen.

8. Celebrating Success—Upscale bar in Toledo, Washington.

The adventure shook my creativity loose just like Stephen had thought it would, and I began writing my book in earnest. The book I wrote is now in your hands.

The Jazz Singer

In 2016, a month after skydiving, I began to wonder what else I could do. My drive to learn self-improvement skills came from my belief that you don't need a problem in front of you to become a better person.

I had unlearned limiting beliefs about myself throughout my life, but even at age sixty-eight, I still felt there was more I could unlearn. I had always wanted to be a jazz singer, so I set out to change other people's beliefs that I couldn't sing.

First, I selected Daryl to be my buddy, since we had similar musical skills and experience. After jumping out of a plane together, I knew I could count on him for support and encouragement. He wanted to learn how to sing, too, and thought it was a good fear to tackle on his next birthday.

Next, we enlisted Shirley to be our vocal coach. Shirley was a local vocal teacher who worked with Daryl. She volunteered to help us. Shirley was encouraging but also firm in her belief that if Daryl and I were serious about singing, we needed to perform in front an audience.

Finally, I created a stage name, Luella Mellini, to fit the persona I wished to create. When I was young, my sister and I had shared a doll we named Luella after our aunt who gave it to us. It felt good to draw from the time in my life when I performed on the hearth of my grandfather's fireplace, especially since "Lou" is my middle name. "Mellini" came about because my maiden name was "Mell" and because I had recently discovered that I have Italian ancestors. It was easy to imagine that during the Jazz Age in Italy, a singer named Luella Mellini existed: Luella was a polished jazz singer with a sultry voice and nerves of steel. She was also funny and joyous, loving each moment on stage.

Daryl and I took lessons together each Wednesday, and Shirley taught us the basics of breath control and pitch. She didn't let us fall back on our fears but gently guided us to gain confidence with each progressively more difficult song. I tried practicing at home, but when my dog, Rickec, started barking while I sang, I started practicing singing in the car along with my CDs. Sometimes I sang while I drove around doing errands, and sometimes I pulled into a waterfront park on the west bay of Olympia. The longer drives gave me a chance to really push myself and take more risks than I could even with my coach.

After ten months of daily practice, we scheduled a concert for forty family members and close friends to celebrate our hard work. When we were planning the concert, I told Daryl and Shirley that I had only one requirement: none of the guests would have professional musical talent. I made one exception for the church pianist because she was the wife of a friend from the Rotary Club, and I didn't want her to be left out. We hired Joe, Daryl's son and a professional pianist, to accompany us.

Daryl wanted to sing Elvis's "Can't Help Falling in Love" for his wife, and prepared other pop songs like Rod Stewart's "Have I Told You Lately That I Love You?" Gordon Lightfoot's "If You Could Read My Mind," and Leonard Cohen's "Hallelujah."

I chose a type of sentimental song called "torch songs." The lyrics for torch songs typically focus on unrequited or lost love, and the music is written for a sultry voice filled with emotion. I borrowed a black top, pants, and a glittery gold jacket from Shirley, and she did my makeup and hair to match.

As I transformed into Luella, I felt different. No longer was I with a group or even skydiving in tandem. Instead, I was going solo. Where Kathy lacked courage, Luella oozed confidence and sensuality. With my sultry voice, I owned the stage. My flaring eyes were sensual instead of startling.

Shirley sat in the front row, and I gave a one-minute intro to each of my five songs. Like I learned from Red Kelly, my intros were designed to be both self-deprecating and funny. I started my set with "Stormy Weather," then sang "Georgia." Next, I sang "Come Rain or Come Shine" followed by "I Didn't Know What Time It Was."

When the audience laughed at my stories and jokes, I felt they were laughing *with* me instead of *at* me as I had feared in the past. When I sang "Fever" as my finale, I encouraged the audience to join in by singing the word "Fever" back to me. Elated, I bowed in gratitude for their standing ovation.

A month later, I attended a concert featuring vocalists Dee Brown and Jamie Jenson. One of the past performers at our house concerts, Dee had heard of my successful first concert and invited me to sing "Fever" for their audience. I was astonished, but accepted her invitation, something I would not have dreamed of doing a year prior.

With Hans Bremmer on piano and Clipper Anderson on bass, I felt held and safe on stage as Luella Mellini. For the first time, I felt what all the other jazz musicians I had enjoyed hearing had felt. Performing that night gave me a glimpse of what Jack had felt playing with great bands all those years.

I learned how hard a vocalist works, from choosing the right songs for my vocal range to practicing, finding good backup musicians, and all the way down to choosing the right venue for the audience I wanted to reach.

As you can see, I once again used the eight key elements for creating *adversitunities* to strengthen the new vision I had of my best life.

1. Detailed Goal Statement—Sing jazz.

2. List of Skills and Resources—Choosing the right songs. Learning how to sing. Developing confidence in singing.

3. Ally —Daryl.

4. Expert—Shirley, vocal coach.

5. Vision of Future Self—Someone brave enough to sing jazz in front of others.

6. Specific Goal Date—Ten months after starting singing lessons.

7. Supporting Others—Daryl.

8. Celebrating Success—Giving a concert to forty friends. Accepting an invitation to perform with local jazz greats.

Learning to sing and perform in front of others was the fulfillment of a lifelong dream, one I didn't think was possible when I was a child. With persistence and determination, though, I found the resources and support I needed to manifest the next stage of my best life.

**What unfulfilled lifelong dream do you
have that may seem impossible now?**

**What can you do today to start moving
toward making it possible?**

_____

_____

_____

_____

_____

_____

_____

_____

_____

_____

_____

_____

_____

_____

"There is nothing more fulfilling and thrilling than discovering yourself to be a stronger person than you ever dreamed yourself capable of being."

— Karen Salmansohn

CHAPTER 13

METHOD FOR A NEW MOTTO

"Doubt kills more dreams than failure ever will."

— Suzy Kassem

As you have learned from my story, adversity ran my life and determined how I lived from a young age. However, once I implemented strategies to overcome stuttering, my life opened up, and I experienced the success I had desired so long.

In the introduction of this book, I talked about five key strategies for changing difficult life circumstances into *adversitunities*:

1. Positive Thinking

2. Support from Others

3. Perseverance

4. Problem-Solving

5. Expressing Gratitude

I hope by sharing my story and offering prompts through-out this book, I have illustrated how important these strategies are in creating the life you dream of. When faced with a challenge, struggle, or setback, remember my first motto, *"There must be some way."* This will help you get back on the path to changing adversity into opportunity—creating *adversitunities* to reclaim your power and reboot your life.

As Chapter 1 pointed out, **adversity is part of life**. Everywhere we look, we see unmistakable struggles causing others pain. If we ignore the difficulties in our lives, they will only persist. Although pain is inevitable, suffering is optional. We can end our suffering by changing our perspective on life and the challenges we face. This shift in perspective is the first step to **Positive Thinking.**

Positive Thinking is mandatory to creating an indomitable spirit. Our brains, however, are programmed by our experiences to respond to negative emotions by shutting off the outside world, narrowing our vision, and limiting the options around us. In a way, our brains keep us safe by preventing us from taking risks; however, this habit often develops when we are young and not as strong as we are later. The first step in shifting our perspective is realizing we are living with a destructive mindset, a mindset reinforced by negative self-talk. Maybe these phrases sound familiar to you:

- I can't do it.
- I must be perfect.
- I'm not worthy.
- I must not make mistakes.
- I'm not good enough.
- I'm always wrong.
- I'm an idiot.
- Everyone is smarter than I am.
- I can't do anything right.
- I will never succeed.

Our negative thoughts might be things other people said about us as a child or ways we coped with stressors over which we had no control. The thoughts might have even protected us from taking risks we couldn't handle at the time, and as we grew up, we did not know we could release these negative ideas. The thoughts became a motto, a repeated statement or slogan, that defined our identity, experiences, and actions.

We can change our lives by adopting a new motto, because the motto becomes the foundation of a positive attitude, one that empowers us and changes adversity into opportunity. As my story illustrates, my motto, "*There must be some way*," propelled me forward to find new solutions and take positive actions that led me to success in business, love, and community service. The motto, "What others think of me is none of my business," is another impactful phrase that has helped me over the years. By not allowing others' self-limiting opinions to influence me, I can work on being the best me instead of trying to become someone based on another person's experiences and expectations.

You are welcome to adopt one of my mottos or one you've heard before, like "*Carpe diem*," a Latin phrase meaning "Seize the day." You can reassure yourself with phrases like, "Every day is a second chance," or "This too shall pass." Here are a few others:

"One person can make a difference."

— Margaret Mead, anthropologist

"Big journeys begin with small steps."

— Lydia Sweatt, Success.com

"I am enough."

— Rosetta Thurman, Happyblackwoman.com

"Don't let the fear of striking out hold you back."

— Babe Ruth, baseball legend

"It is never too late to be what you might have been."

— George Eliot, novelist

"If we did all the things we are capable of, we would literally astound ourselves."

— Thomas A. Edison, inventor

"Whether you think you can, or you think you can't— you're right."

— Henry Ford, inventor

Think about the phrases that keep you from succeeding….
Now, imagine if a friend said those things about themselves. What
would you tell them to help them feel better? Your response might
help you create a new motto for yourself. Start with the phrase "I
am."

If you feel afraid to speak, your motto could be: I am a
confident, courageous, energized communicator.

If change feels overwhelming: I am resilient and adaptable.

If mistakes feel like failure: I am creative and can find new
ways of doing things.

If you feel unloved: I am loving and loveable.

If you feel inadequate: I am capable of finding support and
resources.

Try to keep the motto under ten words so it's easy to remember.

What motto would you like to adopt?

_____

_____

_____

_____

A negative thought can become a limiting belief in a short time or over many years and many repetitions. No matter what, you will need to repeat your new motto as many times as possible for it to become a habit. One technique is to write the motto on a piece of paper and then tape it to your bathroom mirror so you can read it while you prepare for your day. If your motto is short, you might consider having a bracelet made with the phrase so you can see it on your wrist every day.

Writing a phrase down is always better than trying to memorize it right off the bat since it takes time to learn. This is especially true if you are making significant life changes. Plus, everything somehow seems more official once you write it down, whether it's a phrase about what you're thankful for or your strategy for positive thinking. Scientists have found that writing longhand makes deeper connections in the brain than other forms of writing.

You may find it beneficial to write phrases down in a notebook rather than just typing them into a smartphone app. Your notebook can also chronicle how the phrase helps you through your day. Write the phrase and the date at the top of an empty page, and then write a few sentences about how the phrase helped you make better choices that day.

You can write just about anything as long as it is positive. Even if you feel like you had a bad day, strive to write something positive so you can see the silver lining among the clouds of difficulty. After some time, this practice will turn into a habit, and you will instinctively focus on positive, rather than negative, thoughts.

The more you repeat and refer to your motto each day, the more you build your internal resources—an important source of creativity and resourcefulness that can turn adversities into *adversitunities*. **Positive thinking** can generate positive emotions, and the benefits of positive emotions do not just stop after a few minutes. In fact, the biggest benefit of positive emotions is an enhanced ability to build skills and develop resources for use later in life. Barbara Fredrickson's "broaden and build theory of positive emotions" suggests positive emotions broaden your sense of possibility and open your mind, which, in turn, allows you to build new skills and resources that can provide value in other areas.

Even though shifting my thinking was often difficult, my experiences show what can happen when I repeated my motto, *"There must be some way."* Because I believed another way to live, think, and feel was possible, I broadened my sense of possibility, built new skills, and gathered resources to achieve my goals, whether they were to end my stuttering episodes, build a successful business, celebrate the power of jazz music, or mentor others in their own business ventures. The skills built on each other, reinforcing positive thoughts that other ways existed to achieve my dreams. Positive thoughts became positive feelings, which created positive results, and I gained confidence with each risk I took as I built on my experiences.

By cultivating emotional strength, courage, and discipline, we become more resilient in the face of adversity. When we make ourselves aware certain difficulties are inevitable, we can prepare mentally and then confront adversity head-on like a warrior go-ing into battle. A warrior prepares physically and mentally for all possibilities. They know the battle could be ugly, daunting, and grueling, but they are equipped. More often than not, when you are prepared for the worst, the worst does not happen; life is much less severe than anticipated.

Another invaluable inner resource is the faith that everything will work out. Having faith means believing there is always light at the end of the tunnel and knowing whatever setbacks we experience, they "too shall pass." Everything has its place and purpose.

The next key strategy for changing difficult circumstances into *adversitunities* is to **build your external resources**, not just ma-terial resources but also a support system of family and friends. When the going gets tough, we all need encouragement and support. Talking with supportive friends and family eases our anxieties and helps us see our problems from a different perspective. You might be surprised to discover how often a friend has had a similar experience and can help guide you through a difficult time. Even just knowing you have a friend when you need them can be most comforting.

For a very long time, I thought it virtuous to overcome struggles on my own. Then I came to realize the power of receiving support from others. In fact, many people made a difference as I created the life I longed for. Over the decades, I've worked with consultants, coaches from diverse disciplines, therapists, and guides/mentors—all of them provided the emotional and intellectual support I needed when I needed it most. The opportunity to communicate and collaborate with others, whether personal or professional, has often lifted me and given me the strength to conquer another challenge.

List five people who can support you now. Beside each name write one way (emotional, material, intellectual, etc.) they can support you.

1. _____

2. _____

3. _____

4. _____

5. _____

Many types of support people exist, and I have found that each can provide a different resource. Non-professional support people may be friends or colleagues who take an interest in a specific project or in my own general development. They usually fall into three categories, and each category provides a unique resource, so it's good to gather a mix of non-professional support people.

People who have "set the bar" higher than I thought possible for myself provided the **Golden Carrot Effect.** They could see my potential for growth and success far beyond what I could conceive for myself. Their vision of my future was like a golden carrot they dangled in front of me, creating a shining light I could follow. I have had a few people in my life who have created the **Golden Carrot Effect**, like Daryl and Stephen, and I'm forever grateful for their support. People in this role aren't just cheerleaders who tell me they believe in me; these people share with me how my project or goal is a natural extension of the person they know me to be.

Naysayers, on the other hand, were limited in their vision of my potential and would try to convince me I should not or could not accomplish a task, undertake a feat, or overcome a challenge. Although I would not recommend intentionally gathering **naysayers** into your life, if you do have people who hold you to their limited vision, call on your own tenacity to continue and use the opportunity to grow. My natural determination has used others' **naysaying** to spur me on toward completing my goals. When I announced my plans to skydive, my friend declared me a "crazy old lady." Then I became even more committed to doing the jump. People in this role, I've found, are usually speaking out of their own fears and may even secretly wish they could be as confident as I am.

Often, as I moved toward achieving my goals and changing adversities into *adversitunities*, I became discouraged and wondered if the work was worth the time and effort. It can be difficult to maintain the energy needed to complete long-range goals, but **encouragers** along the way helped me keep my optimism and determination. **Encouragers** cheered me on, listened to my dreams, and sometimes offered suggestions to overcome obstacles. Sometimes **encouragers** had the same goals as I did, so we could cheer each other on just like Daryl and I did for each other when we took singing lessons.

List at least one person for each of the following roles.

Golden Carrot Effect: _____

Naysayer: _____

Encourager: _____

Whatever your goals, a professional coach gives you motivation, accountability, and support, while keeping you focused and moving forward from week to week. One of the most common reasons people work with a coach is the feeling of being "stuck"—they're stuck in a job they don't like, stuck in an unsatisfying relationship, or stuck in a life that lacks meaning and purpose. A coach's job is to get you unstuck, and they do this using a number of tools, techniques, and processes designed to help you find what drives you, where you want to go, and the best way to get there.

Personal life coaches differ from professional and athletics coaches because they focus on building interpersonal skills instead of business or sports skills. But the use of the word "coach" in personal development is no accident. A personal life coach is fundamentally no different than a football or tennis coach. A good sports coach will keep you focused on your goal, provide feedback, encourage you when you're feeling frustrated, and make sure you're challenged enough to make real progress from week to week. Likewise, a good personal life coach will help you stay motivated and focused, and will give you objective feedback to help you get farther, faster than you could on your own.

Think carefully about what you are looking for and hope to gain in a coach. Be sure to work with trained professionals with knowledge in your area of focus. I found a speech therapist to support my goal to speak without a stutter, a business consultant to support my goal to succeed as a businesswoman, and Rotary to support my goal to give back to the community.

It's also important to work with coaches who:

- Have been in your position, or a similar position, and have overcome the inherent struggles.
- Are willing to be a sounding board for your struggles.
- Openly share their experiences, both good and bad.
- Are good role models.

- Are known to you personally, since they are familiar with your situation.

- Are not known by you since they can give a different perspective.

- Have empathy for your situation.

As you can see, you will need more than one coach on your support team, which is why I recommend having both a professional coach and a personal coach. Each kind of coach will give you advice you need for each part of your path. A professional coach will help you outline a business or marketing plan, then help you troubleshoot the plan as it unfolds. A personal coach will help you understand how you handle change and risk, then provide advice on how to work within, and later expand on, your capacity to handle situations as you move along your path.

Another good source of support is joining a Mastermind Group—a group of peers with similar goals and a desire to succeed. Napoleon Hill created the idea of the Mastermind Group in his book *The Law of Success* and developed it more fully in his book *Think and Grow Rich*. Members of Mastermind Groups solve problems with input and advice from other members—they receive support from others in the group. By meeting to talk about their challenges, the group taps into the dynamic energy created by the commitment and excitement members bring to the group. Members challenge each other to raise the bar when creating goals and implementing plans. Members brainstorm solutions and support each other with honesty and compassion, thereby becoming important catalysts for growth.

Some Mastermind Groups are called Roundtables and may meet over the course of several months. Ralph Bruksos, the trainer and management consultant who helped me turn my access control products business into a profitable venture, has led an executive Roundtable group for more than twenty years. His Roundtable fosters community connections that have created long-lasting friendships and new projects that would not have come about without his guidance.

Mastermind Groups can be found through Internet searches or social media such as Facebook and MeetUp. Consider going to several introductory sessions before committing to a group to be sure it's a good fit for your goals and personality.

Where are three Mastermind Groups or

similar groups in your area?

How do you contact them?

1. _____

2. _____

3. _____

The next key strategy for changing difficult life circumstances into *adversitunities* is **Perseverance**. While I somewhat agree in principle with Nietzsche's quote, "What does not kill me makes me stronger," I do not necessarily agree with him in practice. For instance, if you do not have enough built-up resilience or experience dealing with difficulty, adversity can crush you. On the other hand, if you do have sufficient resilience, then indeed, adversity will make you stronger. "How so?" you ask. Resilience, like any muscle, is built up gradually and exponentially with repeated exposure to obstacles. If you lack practice in confronting obstacles, including when you choose to avoid them, one traumatic event can stop you in your tracks.

What obstacles do you face today?

_____

_____

_____

_____

Sometimes I have become discouraged when I could not learn something new quickly enough. My discouragement became negative thinking and then despair if I was not careful. I would lose confidence in my plans and resources; then my positive thinking practices would slip. I recovered my momentum toward my goals by remembering the vision I had for myself and my future. Remembering my vision inspired me to think positively once again, to remember my motto, *"There must be some way,"* and to widen my perspective once again. Then I would turn to my support system and revisit stories of people who had overcome adversity. Their stories motivated me to try again. I may have fallen many times, but I also stood up each time. Just like the actress Julie Andrews said, "Perseverance is failing nineteen times and succeeding the twentieth."

Even though I don't consider myself particularly lucky or smarter than anyone else, I do believe I am persistent and determined. Perseverance is an inner reserve of energy created by **positive thinking** and is reinforced by practice. These steps have helped me strengthen my resilience and **perseverance** over many years:

1. Believe success can be yours.
2. Write down your desire in full detail.
3. Create a visual reminder of your goal.
4. Remind yourself of the importance of your goals.
5. See obstacles as temporary and surmountable.

Determination is the strength to act on the energy created by **positive thinking**. Without action, thoughts produce limited results. These steps have helped me act with determination over many years:

1. Set goals that stretch you but are attainable, challenging but realistic.
2. Set short-term, enjoyable, doable goals you can work with others on.

3. Break down the task, setting smaller goals that build to the main goal. A great and difficult task can seem impossible. To succeed, work on smaller chunks every day.

4. Remember, *"There must be some way."* Don't take "no" for an answer.

When we begin to create positive change, it's important to remember we can become overwhelmed by the ensuing changes. If we try to make too many changes at once, we diffuse our energy and become discouraged. To overcome adversity and live the best life you can envision, focus on one or two problems you want to overcome.

Name two problems you struggle with:

1. _____

_____

2. _____

_____

Choose one of the problems you listed, and

explain why you want to overcome it:

_____

_____

_____

_____

_____

_____

How will life change when you overcome

this particular problem?

_____

_____

_____

_____

_____

_____

What resources and support will you need to overcome this particular problem?

_____

_____

_____

_____

_____

_____

_____

Brainstorm possible solutions or ways to address the problem.

1. _____

_____

2. _____

_____

3. _____

_____

4. _____

_____

5. _____

_____

6. _____

_____

7. _____

_____

8. _____

_____

9. _____

_____

10. _____

_____

A number of years ago, after I retired, I struggled to find my purpose. After studying *Strengthfinders 2.0* by Tom Rath, I learned I am passionate about inspiring others and having a peaceful life. From that insight, I decided to set a goal for myself to live my best life in a peaceful way that also inspired others to live their best lives.

Describe what your best life would look and feel like.

_____

_____

_____

_____

_____

_____

_____

_____

_____

_____

The exploration of your issues and the description of your best life you just wrote could be the bones of a powerful life vision statement—a statement that could help you **persevere**. This description can illuminate your way in periods of darkness and help you change your life in ways you might not otherwise have felt strong enough to make.

Go back and reread the goal statement you wrote in Chapter 1. Does it reflect what you want to achieve now that you understand what *adversitunity* means? If not, write a new Goal Statement.

Create a goal statement based on the

vision you have for your life:

_____

_____

_____

_____

_____

_____

_____

_____

_____

_____

_____

_____

_____

_____

_____

"Fall seven times, stand up eight."

— Japanese proverb

In other words, never quit. I'm not telling you it is going to be easy; I am telling you it is going to be worth it. Taking the steps toward your goals will keep you motivated because you will see the progress. Encountering obstacles and unforeseen circumstances is part of the journey, and with a supportive community, you can achieve your dreams—and more.

The next key strategy for changing difficult life circumstances into *adversitunities* is **Problem Solving**. Take inspiration and learn from others who have dealt successfully with adversity. Many inspiring stories exist of people who overcame seemingly insurmountable odds. They triumphed over adversity, going on to live successful, productive lives instead of surrendering to challenges. As I mentioned before, mastermind groups are excellent sources for both inspiration and ideas on how to solve problems encountered as you move toward your goals.

You could also look to historical figures who overcame challenges. Hellen Keller was a happy baby with a bright future until she was struck deaf and blind by a childhood illness. For years, she suffered violent rages and was unable to speak, let alone learn how to cope with her life. Her parents struggled to find her help until Anne Sullivan, a young teacher fresh from the Perkins School for the Blind, arrived. With great patience and persistence, Sullivan taught Keller sign language and how to speak. Keller went on to study at Radcliffe College, to write her autobiography and over 400 speeches and essays, and to become one of the foremost activists for women's rights and the rights of the disabled. People who worked with and encountered Keller found her boundless optimism and courage inspiring, and many believed she saved the lives of those who would have given up had they not heard her story.

Stephen Hawking was a brilliant physicist and mathematician with a bright future ahead of him when he was diagnosed with ALS, a form of motor neuron disease, shortly after his twenty-first birthday. Even though his health slowly deteriorated, forcing him to rely on a wheelchair for mobility and special software to replicate speech, he continued to develop mathematical principles to describe the way our universe functions. His work proved, and went beyond, Albert Einstein's general theory of relativity, and Hawking's later work provided insights into quantum mechanics, the properties of black holes, and the boundaries of time and space. His life also went beyond science; he married and had three children and, later, three grandchildren. Even though the life expectancy of ALS patients is two to five years, Hawking lived to be seventy-six years old.

Many articles online show the steps to solving problems, whether in the workplace or in personal relationships. Methods to solve problems usually include identifying the problem, listing pos-sible solutions, and evaluating if a solution worked. The number of steps isn't as important as learning what did and did not work in the process. If a solution works, it also can be used over and over again. Solutions that use few resources and are flexible are typically the most successful. One method to solve a problem looks like this:

1. **Identify the Problem**—Albert Einstein once said, "If I were given one hour to save the planet, I would spend fifty-nine minutes defining the problem and one minute resolving it." Knowing what the actual problem *is* can be the trickiest step. As in the example of the house with pests, the prob-lem could be the house (located near a habitat known for mosquitos, poor window seals, lack of screens) or the pests (too many mosquitos). Something important to identify is whether there actually is a problem in the first place. Then, can you find a solution for it? If not, the problem may be something different than what you initially thought.

2. **Gather Information**—Clarity leads to solutions. If you are not clear about the situation, you can't solve it. Gather-ing information includes understanding all the parts of the

problem and analyzing the best way to go about solving it. In the example, it might be cheaper and easier to seal the windows, but it might be easier and better for the environment to stop using pesticides that kill the bats that eat the mosquitos. Solutions may need to be combined to achieve the best results in the shortest time.

3. **Implement Solution**—This step can often cause the most anxiety because of the risks involved. Much like how I felt jumping out of a perfectly good airplane, the solution you discover may be scary. Feeling anxious is a normal part of the problem-solving process, and patience at this point is extremely important.

4. **Evaluate**—Examining how well a solution worked provides more information about the problem *and* the solution itself. After sealing up the windows of our imaginary home, it would take at least a season to be sure all the holes were plugged. We might find that after a good rain, the sealant starts to fail. Instead of giving up, we find a new sealant and try again. The same can be said for any solution to any problem we come up with that works at first then fails.

Steps can and should be repeated for larger and/or long-term goals. Big goals can be broken down into smaller goals, which makes the process easier to manage and more adaptable to changes that come up along the way. This process works not only for business plans but also personal goals. If a project is really consuming my time and making me anxious, frustrated, or upset, I look at what is troubling me and take actions to improve the situation. By using the strategies listed above, I can make an apparently insurmountable problem into an achievable goal.

What obstacles or problems are keeping
you from achieving your goal?

_____

_____

_____

_____

_____

_____

_____

What are some solutions for overcoming

those obstacles or problems?

Describe one step you can take to solve
one of the problems you've listed:

_____

_____

_____

_____

_____

_____

_____

_____

_____

_____

_____

_____

_____

_____

_____

_____

Breaking down problems into steps and finding solutions for each step can be overwhelming. When I was young, I often felt unlovable but, as an adult, I learned and came to appreciate that I had survived and learned to love myself, even when I made mistakes. I learned to love myself by putting myself first and bolstering my self-esteem. Even though I believe in the power of a good community, it is equally important to learn to be one's own person. Looking to others for constant validation often means trying to live up to their expectations instead of your own. Like having internal persistence and external determination, it's important to create a dynamic balance between self-esteem and external markers of success.

Another idea to keep in mind is that your first solution might not be the best solution. Even if it works in the short-term, you may discover it will only work once or only in a limited way. When I was working to overcome my stuttering, holding my tongue with my fingers or slapping my face worked, but it was impractical to continue doing those things. I needed to work with a special therapist to find better strategies and become the experienced speaker I am today. Failure can be humbling, but it shouldn't be an excuse not to try a different solution based on more information and resources. Being persistent and determined to live the life you want hinges on your ability to let go of how you thought things should be and embrace new, and likely better, possibilities.

The last key strategy for changing difficult life circumstances into *adversitunities* is **Expressions of Gratitude.** Whether given face-to-face, written directly to a person, or jotted in a journal, daily expressions of gratitude will keep your attitude positive, your mind open to possibilities, and your heart calm in the midst of uncertainty. You could start the day with an expression of gratitude to a friend or coworker and end your evening by journaling your thanks.

Gratitude has been on philosophers' minds for thousands of years, but its importance has only been recognized recently. It is a key character strength that anyone can develop.

In the program described in his book *Gratitude Works*, Robert Emmons shares his knowledge from a decade of research on gratitude. In the face of despair, gratitude has the power to bring hope. Gratitude can help us cope with hard times.

Here is how the practice of gratitude works: Think of the worst times in your life; then think about where you are now.

You've survived those bad times, the bad relationships, and the trauma, just like I survived my disastrous first marriage and found love. Remembering the bad can help us appreciate the good we have in our lives now.

Write one or two sentences about a bad situation you experienced:

_____

_____

_____

_____

_____

_____

_____

_____

_____

_____

_____

_____

It's normal to still feel strong emotions about the situation, but those strong emotions can become negative emotions (self-judgments) if you don't reframe the experience. To reframe the experience, in your mind or in your journal, ask yourself these key questions:

What lesson did I learn?

_____

_____

_____

_____

_____

_____

_____

_____

_____

_____

_____

What surprising ability, skill, or piece of knowledge did I gain from that lesson?

_____

_____

_____

_____

_____

_____

_____

_____

_____

_____

_____

_____

_____

_____

_____

How have I moved toward the vision of my best

self because of the experience?

_____

_____

_____

_____

_____

_____

_____

_____

_____

_____

_____

_____

_____

_____

_____

_____

_____

Once you can reframe your experience into a learning experience, you can begin to show gratitude while working on conquering the adversity that experience created.

One great way to show gratitude is to visit someone who has done something important and wonderful for you, but whom you feel you have not properly thanked. Share with that person the benefits you received from knowing them. If an in-person visit isn't possible, write a letter expressing your gratitude for all they have done for you.

A good example of expressing gratitude from my own life happened at a recent Rotary meeting. A visitor spotted one of our members, a retired judge, and approached him during lunch. When she returned to my table, she shared that the judge had given her husband a lecture during his court appearance many years ago, and the incident had turned her husband's life around. My friend was grateful she had the opportunity to share this positive result with the judge.

After the meeting, I met the judge in the parking lot. He was honored to have learned the outcome of his advice. He shared that he rarely knows if he has made a difference with those who appear in his court.

Another way of showing gratitude is to write, in a journal each night, three things for which you are thankful. Since I live in the Northwest, I always give thanks when there is a sunny day. Peacefulness and wellbeing fill my heart as I fall asleep.

What three things are you grateful for today?

1. _____

_____

2. _____

_____

3. _____

_____

"Change is hardest at the beginning, messiest in the middle, and best at the end."

— Robin Sharma

CHAPTER 14

FROM GOALS TO LIVING THE VISION OF YOUR BEST SELF

"Doubt kills more dreams than failure ever will."

— Suzy Kassem

I n this chapter, we will take some of the answers you wrote earlier and revisit them to create your personal plan that will connect the eight key elements for creating *adversitunities*:

1. Detailed Goal Statement

2. List of Skills and Resources

3. Network of Allies

4. Expert

5. Vision of Future Self

6. Specific Goal Date

7. Supporting Others

8. Celebrating Success

Creating a Detailed Goal Statement

A compelling personal vision statement can illuminate our way during periods of darkness. It can inspire us to shed all the stuff that holds us back.

In Chapter 13, you were prompted to choose a problem to overcome, and then to respond to two questions. Look back at your answers to see if they still hold true for you.

Why do you want to overcome the particular problem you identified?

_____

_____

_____

_____

_____

_____

_____

_____

_____

_____

_____

_____

_____

_____

_____

_____

_____

How will your life change if you overcome this particular problem?

_____

_____

_____

_____

_____

_____

_____

_____

_____

_____

_____

_____

_____

_____

_____

_____

You then went on to write a goal statement. Write a new one here based on what you've gleaned from the ideas in this book. Keep it to a short phrase or a single sentence.

Write a goal statement based on the

vision you have for your life:

_____

_____

_____

_____

_____

_____

_____

_____

_____

_____

_____

_____

_____

List of Skills and Resources

In Chapter 2, you wrote a list of your strongest skills and the resources you have to help you reach your goals. Copy them here, and add to them if needed.

What are your strongest skills?

If you can't think of any, ask your life buddy

what they most admire about you.

_____

_____

_____

_____

_____

_____

_____

_____

_____

_____

What resources (big and small) do you have

that will help you reach your goal?

_____

_____

_____

_____

_____

_____

_____

_____

_____

_____

_____

_____

_____

_____

_____

_____

Buddies

Along the way to achieving my goals and creating my best life, I had cheerleaders and companions to help me. Look back at your answer in Chapter 2 to this question:

Who is your life buddy, and how can they support your goal?

_____

_____

_____

_____

_____

_____

_____

_____

_____

_____

_____

_____

You may have thought of other people whom you consider supportive buddies when you responded to the following in Chapter 13:

Name five people who can support you now.

What kind of resources do they provide (emotional, material, intellectual)?

1. _____

2. _____

3. _____

4. _____

5. _____

Sometimes our allies are people we have not met, but who have inspired us, nonetheless. In Chapter 1, you were asked who lives or has lived the kind of life you want to live now.

Write about a person who inspires you:

_____

_____

_____

_____

_____

_____

_____

_____

_____

_____

_____

_____

_____

_____

_____

_____

_____

_____

In Chapter 7, you wrote about two people you admire and their characteristics.

Who are the two people you admire?

1. _____

2. _____

What characteristics do each of the above people

possess that would help you achieve your goals?

_____

_____

_____

_____

_____

_____

_____

_____

_____

_____

All these allies, close by and/or distant in time and space, are people you can draw on for help and ideas. Interact with them often, and let their passions and creativity help you tap into your own passion and creativity more deeply.

Experts

Consulting experts is the best way to gather the skills, knowledge, and experience you need to overcome adversity, set and execute plans for reaching your goals, and create your best life. I have consulted with many experts over the course of my life— from speech therapists to business coaches, skydiving guides, and even a vocal coach. (We talked about professional and personal coaches in Chapter 13.)

Name three places you can find an expert to support your goals.

1. _____

2. _____

3. _____

Once you have found experts to talk to, write their names and contact information here. If you prefer to meet with them in person, be sure to ask if they have an office close to your home. If you are comfortable with calling or emailing, then ask for that contact information, too.

Name three professional coaches who could support your goals.

1. _____

2. _____

3. _____

Name three personal coaches who could support your goals.

1. _____

2. _____

3. _____

I recommend going to a free seminar offered by the coach to see if their personality is a good fit—especially if their courses are expensive. Treat coaching like an investment of both time and money, and be sure you have enough of both to sustain a coaching relationship. If you find yourself limited, go back to your buddies to see if they can help you find the time and/or funds you need to gain the skills and expertise for which you are looking.

Which seminars or workshops could you take?

1. _____

2. _____

3. _____

Earlier in this chapter, you wrote about what you envision your life to be overall. Now narrow your focus to the specific problem you want to change into an *adversitunity*.

What would be the best outcome if you were able to

change your problem into an opportunity?

_____

_____

_____

_____

_____

_____

_____

Now look at the answer you wrote to this question:

What one step can you take to solve

one of the problems you listed?

_____

_____

_____

_____

_____

_____

Specific Goal Date

Look at your calendar, and decide when you are going to take that one step. Make it as soon as possible, within the next thirty days. Tell your allies you are going to take that step by the date you have decided, and then ask them to check on you. Make sure at least three people know about that date.

Write that date here:

_____

It can be easy to set your own goals aside because of other people's expectations. Perhaps you are a parent who needs to take a child to an event. Perhaps you are a person who works odd hours, making it difficult to set time aside for yourself. Perhaps you have a physical condition you are worried may flare up.

Still, put the date on your calendar and work toward keeping that day clear of distractions. If something comes up, reschedule your goal date as soon as you can. If you find yourself rescheduling the date often, then go to your coach to find better ways to stay on track. You are making an important decision to live a better life, so you owe it to yourself to follow through.

Supporting Others

Sometimes it's easier to meet a goal when you are supporting others. This is why I feel service organizations like the Rotary Club can give us the opportunity not only to better our communities but also ourselves. Mastermind groups also provide the opportunity to support others on similar paths to live better lives and increase our own chances of success.

List service or charity organizations that match your goals and values:

_____

_____

_____

_____

_____

List local mastermind groups or Meetups

that match your goals and values:

_____

_____

_____

_____

_____

_____

Set a date for when you will attend a meeting of

one of these service or mastermind groups:

_____

_____

_____

_____

_____

_____

Celebrating Success

The last step to creating *adversitunities* is to set aside time to celebrate successes. When you are starting out, the celebration could be as simple as treating yourself and your ally to coffee or ice cream. Celebrating might look like an exciting Facebook post.

Measure success by whether you did your best to meet your goal by the date you set. If you were not able to, then review the situation with a friend or coach to see if your goal was too ambitious for your skills and available time. Adjust and make new goals. Celebrate each goal you reach.

List fun and meaningful ways to celebrate accomplishing your goals:

_____

_____

_____

_____

_____

_____

Living your best life by changing adversity into *adversitunities* is an ongoing process of discovery and learning. Sometimes the process is hard, and that is when you need your allies, experts, and coaches to take you to the next level. Sometimes it is a fun process, especially when you do something you never imagined possible.

At the beginning of this book, I told you your dreams matter to me, and I believe you can accomplish them with persistence and determination. I hope the stories I have shared will help inspire you to achieve your goals and more.

"And as we let our own light shine, we unconsciously give other people permission to do the same. As we are liberated from our fear, our presence automatically liberates others."

— Marianne Williamson

A FINAL NOTE

"I'm not scared of growing old; I'm just scared
of not achieving everything that I want to do."

— Melanie Laurent

A t the beginning of this book, I gave you some good news and some bad news about the helpless feelings you may have had when you considered all the changes and complexities that make up your life right now.

The bad news: You are not unique.

The good news: You are not alone.

As you have read, over the past seventy years, I've experienced both terrible lows and terrific highs. I've gone from profound stuttering as a child, through failed businesses and a disastrous marriage, to enjoying the love of a great artist and becoming a jazz singer and business mentor. In this final chapter, I want to highlight how important it is to have the internal resources I have talked about ready, to be prepared to implement your best strategies when problems—obstacles, setbacks, and struggles—present themselves.

Around the time I started this book in January 2018, I noticed I was experiencing tremors in my left hand. At first, I thought I was drinking too much coffee. I limited my coffee intake to one cup per day. With no positive results, I stopped consuming coffee entirely.

I made other changes to my lifestyle too, such as reducing my alcohol consumption and adjusting medication dosages, but the tremors grew worse. The first awkward time happened when I was eating lunch; a tremor hit and my Spanish rice ended up on a fellow Rotarian's plate. Dining out became embarrassing; I ended up eating foods I could hold in my hand (lots of hamburgers) and tried getting as much control over the trembling as possible.

The tremors migrated to my right hand, and, when I was tired, I experienced weakness on my right side. I became concerned that I might fall.

After eliminating other possible causes of the trembling, I was diagnosed with Parkinson's disease (PD) by a neurologist, about sixteen months after my first symptoms appeared.

Although I had considered PD a possibility earlier, I was not prepared for the shock of this incurable, progressive, and degenerative reality. For three weeks, I spent most of my time sleeping, wanting to escape this life-changing event.

Then one day, I rallied. I started taking small self-care steps. I shared the news with my family and inner circle of friends, especially those I knew would be there for me as time and PD progressed.

One thought kept nagging at me, though: How do I get out of this predicament?

As I was brushing my teeth one morning, I looked into the mirror. I could not believe what I saw. I appeared to have aged ten years in just three weeks. My green eyes were dull and no longer smiling. I was shocked at the change. I thought I must take action.

"*There must be some way.*"

Then it hit me. *Read your own book.*

I proceeded as I had so many times before. I asked myself: What's the worst thing that can happen? Through research, I found that the end stages could be (but were not always) devastating because of hallucinations, dementia, and being bedridden.

I went to the next step: Check it out. Will that final stage be true for me? Probably not, as I developed PD later in life, and the disease progresses slowly.

I also found support groups where I can share my journey. And I learned exercise regimens and boxing can slow degeneration.

Next, research. I bought books on living with Parkinson's, DVDs for exercise, and downloaded information from the Internet. I continue to explore this subject weekly. There are a number of cutting-edge technologies being developed right now that help us understand this dastardly disease.

Next, a sense of humor. Having been fortunate enough to grow up in a family that finds humor in most anything, I discover at least one aspect at which to laugh each day. Rather than dreading the use of a cane, I am looking forward to purchasing several canes to match my different outfits. And there is often a handsome man who can help me up and down stairs!

My motto continues to be "*There must be some way.*" I have also added "*Carpe diem*" to celebrate each and every day.

Next is finding the support of others. My family, especially my sister Patty, checks in with me frequently to see how I am doing. Friends make sure I am not left in isolation for too long. Their willingness to listen patiently as I describe my latest symptoms is, for right now, the best therapy as I settle into my new routines. One friend reminded me recently that my "encore life" is to be experienced at my best level, and that idea has spurred me on.

Throughout this book, I have shared stories from my own life and asked you questions about yours. I hope seeing how my experiences and strategies worked for me might show you how they could work in your life. I hope you see how to apply the techniques to overcoming your obstacles. And that you, too, will discover your own ways to change adversity into *adversitunity*, just as I am doing once again.

The strategies I have shared in this book have brought me to such wonderful places in my life, and I would love to hear about what they bring for you. I encourage you to share your success with me via email. Always remember the bad news is you are not special, but the good news is you are not alone. Keep pushing because there must be some way.

Kathryn Perciful

Kathryn Perciful
Kathy@ThereMustBeSomeWay.com
Olympia, WA

"One day you will tell your story of how you've overcome what you're going through now, and it will become part of someone else's survival guide."

— The Women's Center

RESOURCES

Best Self Decks—*Decision Deck, Edison Deck, WordSmith Deck.*
      Best Self. https://bestself.co/

Dale Carnegie. *How to Stop Worrying and Start Living.*

Dale Carnegie. *How to Win Friends and Influence People.*

Dale Carnegie Training: https://www.dalecarnegie.com/en

Napoleon Hill. *The Law of Success.*

Napoleon Hill. *Think and Grow Rich.*

Ralph Bruksos. *It's Time to Move On.*

Toastmasters International: Toastmasters.org

ABOUT THE AUTHOR

Kathryn Perciful has spent her life trying to turn adversities into opportunities, leading to her coining the term "adversitunities."

Kathy's adversities began at a young age when she developed a stutter and tried to compensate for it in various ways. At times, it held her back in her career, but living her motto, "There must be some way," she always found a way to work around it and eventually overcome it.

Kathy has worked in a variety of roles in various businesses ranging from alarm systems to the petroleum business. Her marriage to the legendary jazz artist Jack Perciful resulted in her becoming a concert organizer and even dabbling in a career as a jazz singer.

Now in her seventies, Kathy's diagnosis of Parkinson's disease resulted in her taking once more the advice in her own book about how to overcome adversity. Today, Kathy is living her "encore life" as she continues to find creative ways to turn her adversities into opportunities, share her story, and enjoy every moment.